Instant Pot Cookbook for Two

Instant Pot Cookbook for Two

The Best Easy, Delicious and Healthy Recipes to cook in Instant Pot Recipes Cookbook for Two.

Emily Lovano

Copyright@2019 by Published in the United States by Emily Lovano

All Rights Reserved.

No a part of this publication or the knowledge in it should be quoted from or reproduced in any kind by suggests that like printing, scanning, photocopying or otherwise while not previous written permission of the copyright holder.

Disclaimer and Terms of Use:

Consistent efforts have been made to make sure that the information provided in this book is accurate and complete. However, the author or publisher doesn't guarantee the accuracy of the information, graphics, and text contained within the e-Book mainly due to the rapidly changing nature of research, science, known and unknown facts on the internet. The author and publisher are not held responsible for errors, contra interpretation or any omission regarding the subject. This e-Book is presented mainly for informational and motivational purposes only. This book is presented solely for Cooking and informational purposes only.

TABLE OF CONTENTS

- Introduction 10
- Why is the instant pot perfect for two? 11
  - Perfect size: 11
  - Harmony in the kitchen: 11
  - Easy clean-up: 11
  - Great for small kitchens: 11
- Parts & Accessories of the Instant Pot 11
- The Buttons 12
- Instant Pot Benefits 13
  - The only kitchen appliance you need: 13
  - Easy to use: 13
  - Gets dinner on the table…quickly 14
  - Multipurpose: 14
  - Healthy food: 14
- Tips for Cooking in Instant pot 14
  - Keep it simple at the start: 14
  - Remember added time: 14
  - Get extra parts: 15
  - Clean it regularly: 15
- Breakfast Recipes 16
  - Egg Croissants: 17
  - Broccoli Egg Morning: 18
  - Broccoli Cheese Omelet: 19
  - Jar Breakfast: 20
  - Vanilla Peach Oats: 21
  - Pecan Pie Oatmeal: 22
  - Berry Chia Oats: 23
  - Potato Ham Breakfast Casserole: 24

Boiled Eggs: 25

Ham Sausage Quiche: 26

Millet Porridge: 27

Chia Spiced Rice Pudding: 28

Cheesy Bacon Oats: 29

Crunchy Cinnamon Toast Rice Pudding: 30

Bacon Egg Mystery Muffins: 31

Chicken Recipes 32

Barbecue Chicken: 33

Tangy Cranberry Turkey: 34

Sweet Chicken Retreat: 35

Creamy Chicken with Mushroom: 36

Noodle Cream Chicken: 37

Pina Colada Chicken: 38

Oregano Pasta Chicken: 39

Sweet BBQ Chicken Wings: 40

Turkey Legs with Gravy: 41

Rosemary Wine Chicken: 42

Cacciatore Chicken: 43

Oregano Pasta Chicken: 44

Chicken Olives Feast: 45

Braised Chicken with Parsley and Capers: 46

Chicken Parmesan Risotto: 47

Beef, Pork & Lamb Recipes 48

Beef Bourguignon: 49

Artichoke Mayo Beef: 50

Balsamic Soy Beef Roast: 51

Corned Beef with Cabbage: 52

Mozzarella Beef Lasagna: 53

Parmesan & Honey Pork Roast: 54

Creamy Pork Treat: 55

Enchilada Pork tacos: 56

Pork Tenderloin Teriyaki: 57

Worcestershire Honey Pork: 58

Braised Lamb Shanks: 59

Squash Wine Lamb Meal: 60

Spinach Lentil Lamb: 61

Braised Lamb with Tomatoes and Carrots: 62

Spiced Potato Lamb Dinner: 63

Seafood & Fish Recipes 64

Ginger-Lemon Haddock: 65

Olive Cod Mystery: 66

Tomato Herbed Fish: 67

Wild Alaskan Cod: 68

Buttery Shrimp Paella: 69

Glazed Salmon: 70

Mussels Tomatino: 71

Wine Braised Calamari: 72

Black Bean and Rice Shrimp: 73

Orange Scallop Mania: 74

Fish Curry: 75

White Wine Haddock: 76

Honey Lemon Salmon: 77

Perfectly Steamed Crab Legs 78

Spicy Saucy Crab Cakes: 79

Vegetables Recipes 80

Butternut Squash Risotto: 81

Wholesome Asparagus Appetizer: 82

- Chickpea Tofu Pasta: 83
- Cauliflower and Sweet Potato Mash: 84
- Eggplant Olive Crush: 85
- Rice & Lentils with Veggies: 86
- Cheesy Asparagus: 87
- Parmesan Spinach Pasta: 88
- Root Vegetable Mash: 89
- Apple Cabbage Delight: 90
- Curried Edamame: 91
- Bacon Honey Sprouts: 92
- Mixed Veggie Rice Meal: 93
- Mushroom Cauliflower Risotto: 94
- Parmesan Zoodles: 95

Soups & Stews Recipes 96
- Pork Soup: 97
- Chicken Spiced Tropical Soup: 98
- Crab Sherry Soup: 99
- Creamy Wild Rice mushroom Soup 100
- Chicken Mushroom Garlic Soup: 101
- Marinara Turkey Soup: 102
- Chicken Pasta Soup: 103
- Beef & Potato Stew: 104
- Cream Chicken Stew: 105
- Weeknight Easy Pork Stew: 106
- Mexican Bean Beef Stew: 107
- Spicy Sausage Stew: 108
- Beef and Barley Stew: 109
- Chili Honey Pork Stew: 110
- Lamb Leg Stew with Cinnamon and Dates: 111

CONCLUSION: 113

Introduction

Instant pot cooking is the future in the kitchen! More people all over the world adopt this cooking method every day! It became popular over the last few years and it has gained millions of fans!
Instant pots are the most useful tools you can use in the kitchen these days! They allow you to cook some of the most delicious and flavored dishes ever in no time!
You can forget about using pans, pots, stoves, and ovens! Instant pots replace all these kitchen tools. They will make cooking a lot more fun!
You will soon see that an instant pot is the only kitchen appliance you need and you will end up loving it.
Now that you are convinced that an instant pot is such an amazing tool, let's find out the real reason why we developed this cookbook. We thought you could use an instant pot cooking guide that could teach you how to make the best dishes for you and your loved one!
Therefore, if you fell in the mood for making a succulent and flavored meal for you and your partner, you can check out our cookbook! Try making magical meals for two using just your instant pot!
Trust us! It will be an epic experience!
Your beloved are thus happy and happy and you'll become a begin within the kitchen!
So, what are you still doing here? Haven't you started your culinary journey yet?
Let's get to work and prepare the best instant pot dishes for two!
Have a lot of fun cooking with your instant pot!

Why is the instant pot perfect for two?

Perfect size:
With your instant pot, you can make enough for just the two of you to eat for one meal…. With a few leftovers for you take for lunch or another meal

Harmony in the kitchen:
No more arguing about whose turn it is to make dinner. The instant pot is so easy to use; you'll both want to impress the other with the delicious meal recipes in my book.

Easy clean-up:
Clean-up in the kitchen is super easy with the instant pot. You'll only have one pot to clean! You can wash it with warm soapy water, or even-easier-toss it into the dishwasher. Less time in the kitchen is more time doing something else you both want to do.

Great for small kitchens:
The instant pot is ideal for a small kitchen. When you're not using it, you can store it away in a cupboard. Or you can leave it on the counter for your next meal. Remember, when you have an instant pot with all those functions, you can get rid of all those other appliances that are just taking up valve space in your kitchen.

Parts & Accessories of the Instant Pot

Now that you have a handle on what your multicooker can do, it is worth knowing how it's set up, what parts it comes with—and any additional items you need. Before you start, though, you will want to ready your multicooker's manual. Each one is totally different, but there are a number of parts every model should have.

1. Outer body: This contains the brain of the appliance, with a display panel and various buttons for setting the functions. The outer body is what heats up when you turn the machine on. The inner pot sits within the cooker's outer body. Never put food directly in the outer body if the inner pot is not there.

2. Sealing ring: this silicone gasket surrounds the lid and helps seal steam into the pot. Sealing rings can absorb the odor of strongly scented foods, like garlic, ginger, and onions, during the cooking process. Some people like to buy extra sealing rings to use solely for delicate dishes, such as custards or plain rice. Always wash the sealing rings after use.

Steamer rack or basket: this sits within the inner pot and keeps food raised higher than the liquid once you don't wish it submerged.

3. Lid: the lid covers the pot, keeping in steam. It needs to be locked into place before the pressure cooking function can be turned on. Some multicookers have removable lids, while others have lids that are secured to the body of the pot on a hinge.

4. Steam valve: found on the lid, this valve allows the pot to build pressure or to release it. It has a sealing (locked) position and a venting (open) position. When using the pressure cooking function, the valve should be in the sealing position, or the pressure won't build. One common mistake for new multicooker user is not properly sealing the vent. When mistreatment the slow preparation operates, it must be in the venting position.

5. Pressure valve: this metal valve indicates when the instant pot is pressurized and when it is not. It wills pop-up when the instant pot reaches pressure, and drop down when the pressure is released. You may not be able to see the valve pop-up or down if it is hidden under a plastic cover, which is sometimes the case depending on the model of your instant pot.

6. Condensation collector: this plastic cup clips onto the outer body of the pot, catching any condensation released during slow cooking. You don't need to use it while pressure cooking as the steam is contained in the appliance.

Inner pot: a stainless-steel or non-stick pot, this is where the food cooks. It should be removed for cleaning.

ACCESSORIES:
These items aren't necessary for victimization your multicooker, however they're useful: aluminum foil for covering pans and, making slings for lifting dish dishes and cake pans out of the pot; a 6-or 7-inch spring form cake pan, for cheesecakes and other cakes; steamer basket and racks; a non-stick insert, for making rice with trading (a crisp, golden rice dish) and other probably sticky dishes; and a glass lid, for seeing the progress of our food once slow preparation.

The Buttons

There is a manual setting that you can use with your instant pot push of a button. In some instant pots, there is even a time that wills common buttons.

- **Manual:** you use this setting if you want to adjust the pressure and cooking time. Most recipes use the manual setting.
- **Sauté:** this allows you to adjust from frying to simmer. You use it to heat foods and thicken sauces.
- **Slow cook:** you use this to use your instant pot as you would a slow cooker. To use this setting turn the pressure release to the venting position.
- **Keep warm/cancel:** this will cancel your setting while still keeping your food warm.
- **Soup**: you'll see this for soups, which cooks for forty minutes at high pressure. You can still adjust the time manually.
- **Meat/ stew:** this cooks at high pressure for thirty-five minutes. You can adjust the cooking time manually.
- **Bean chili:** this cooks at high pressure for a half hour. You can adjust the cooking time manually.
- **Rice:** this prepares rice, and you cannot adjust the cooking time manually.
- **Poultry:** this cooks oatmeal and other poultry for fifteen-minute at high pressure. You can adjust the cooking time manually.
- **Porridge:** this cooks oatmeal and porridge at high pressure for twenty minutes. You can adjust the cooking time manually.
- **Multigrain:** this cooks at high pressure for forty minutes, but the cooking time can be adjusted manually.
- **Steam:** you use this to steam foods, including vegetables, using a steamer basket. It cooks at high pressure for ten minutes.

Instant Pot Benefits

The only kitchen appliance you need:

It's expensive to have a variety of different appliance that takes up a lot of room in your kitchen….and then there are all the pots pans. with all the functions the instant pot can perform, it's an economic investment that will make more room in your kitchen cupboards when you get rid of the rice cooker and steamer that are just taking up kitchen space.

Easy to use:

Using the instant pot is as easy as pressing a few buttons. No more complicated recipes that take you forever to read through and then just as long to make. Now the instant pot does all the work for you. And my recipes are so easy to follow, without a lot of steps for you to work your way through. The instant pot is perfect for couples who aren't professional chefs but who still want to enjoy a great tasting meal at home.

Gets dinner on the table...quickly

The instant pot slashes cooking time, so dinner is ready in on time. Using pressure and high temperatures, food cooks quickly and efficiently. You can throw everything together and have a meal prepared in the blink of an eye. Once you use the instant pot, you won't be able to live without it! You'll be able to cook roasts ribs in less than an hour!

Multipurpose:

With so many different instant pot functions you can make different and exciting dishes every night of the week. Creamy soups, delicious stews, juicy roasts, and screamer vegetables. No matter what you're craving. You'll find just the right recipe in my book

Healthy food:

The instant pot lets you safely cook healthy meals. By pressure cooking at high temperature, food cooks in its juices, keeping both flavors and nutrients right in the pot. When you're focusing on eating right, cooking for two has never been so easy the instant pot is completely safe to use. When food is prepared, the instant pot automatically releases pressure to lower the temperature. Or you can control the pressure by using the release valve.

Tips for Cooking in Instant pot

While it does many thighs with ease, the instant pot is especially well-suited towards the creation of soups, chilis, and stews made from scratch. Its ability to soften up unsoaked beans, while all the other ingredients cook, is a real bonus for busy people. It can also turn even the toughest cut of meat into fall-off-the-bone perfection in very short order, which makes it ideal for things such as spare ribs.
Make sure you use enough liquid when you're cooking, and don't try anything in it because oil can damage the system.

Keep it simple at the start:
It's going to take you a while to familiarize yourself with the variety of function with which an instant pot is equipped. If you are a first- time user, you need to keep things simple. Rather than trying your hand at a complex cooking method, try something easy first, like boiling eggs or earning up to a dish.

Remember added time:
It will about 10 minutes for your instant pot to come to pressure. For example, if it takes 20 minutes of cooking at high pressure, then you'll need to add 10 minutes to the total cooking time. You will also need to add 10 to 20 minutes for natural pressure release (depending on how much food you have in the pot). Even a quick pressure can take a few minutes. You don't need to add cook time if you're using the slow cooker or sauté option.

Because of the time lag involved in both starting and stopping the pressure cooking process. Fish and seafood have to be treated with particular care since many of these ingredients can turn either mushy or rubbery if overcooked.

Get extra parts:

The instant pot comes with a stainless steel inner pot; however, getting an extra inner pot could help you to prepare two different dishes. Also, if you use the instant pot quite often, then you will always have one inner pot available for use while the other is being cleaned in the dishwasher.
You can also cook with different lids, you actually get a glass lid, which is similar to slow cooker lid. You can use this lid when you're using the sauté or slow cooker functions. The glass lid cannot be used for the pressure cooking function.

Clean it regularly:

Just because it takes less time to cook, does not mean that it doesn't require frequent cleaning. Fortunately, this appliance is very to clean, as the inner pot easily detachable. Make it a habit to clean your instant pot after each use.

Breakfast Recipes

Egg Croissants:

Serves: 2
Preparation Time: 5 minutes
Cooking Time: 8 minutes
Macros per serving:

Calories: 482
Protein: 21.0 grams
Fat: 29.9 grams
Carbohydrates: 31.5 grams

Ingredients:

- 4 large eggs
- Salt and pepper to taste
- 4 slices of cooked bacon, broken into small pieces
- 5 tablespoons shredded cheddar cheese
- 1 green scallion, diced
- 4 croissants

How to make it:

1. Place a steamer basket inside the instant pot and pour in 1½ cups water.
2. Whip the eggs in a bowl. Add the bacon pieces, cheese, and scallion to the eggs. Mix well.
3. Divided the mixture into 4 muffin cups. Transfer the filled muffin cups onto the steamer basket.
4. Shut the lid and cook at high pressure for 8 minutes.
5. When the cooking is complete, do a natural pressure release for 5 minutes. Quick-release the remaining pressure.
6. Lift the muffin cups out the instant pot.
7. Slice 4 croissants in half and stuff with the muffin cup content.

Broccoli Egg Morning:

Serves: 2
Preparation Time: 5-8 minutes
Cooking Time: 5 minutes
Macros per serving:

Calories: 376
Protein: 23 grams
Fat: 28 grams
Carbohydrates: 9 grams

Ingredients:

- 3 eggs, whisked
- ½ cup broccoli florets
- A pinch garlic powder
- 2 tablespoons tomatoes
- 1 clove garlic, minced
- ½ small yellow onion, chopped
- ½ red bell pepper, chopped
- 2 tablespoons cheese, grated
- A pinch chili powder
- 2 tablespoons onions
- 2 tablespoons parsley
- Pepper and salt as needed

How to make it:

1. Take your 3-quart instant pot; open the top lid. Plug it and turn it on.
2. Open the top lid; grease inside cooking surface using a cooking spray.
3. In a bowl, whisk the eggs.
4. Add the remaining ingredients except for the cheese. Season with pepper and salt.
5. In the cooking pot area, add the mixture.
6. Close the top lid and seal its valve.
7. Press "STEAM" setting. Adjust cooking time to 5 minutes.
8. Allow the recipe to cook for the set cooking time.
9. After the set cooking time ends, press "CANCEL" and then press "QPR (Quick Pressure Release)".
10. Instant pot wills quickly releaser the pressure.
11. Open the top lid; add the cooked recipe mix in serving plates. Top with the cheese.
12. Serve and enjoy!

Broccoli Cheese Omelet:

Serves: 2
Preparation Time: 5 minutes
Cooking Time: 5 minutes
Macros per serving:

Calories: 389
Protein: 24.3 grams
Fat: 28.7 grams
Carbohydrates: 9.8 grams

Ingredients:

- 1 clove garlic, minced
- ½ small yellow onion, chopped
- ½ red bell pepper, chopped
- 3 eggs, whisked
- ½ cup broccoli florets
- A pinch garlic powder
- 2 tablespoons tomatoes, diced
- 2 tablespoons onions, diced
- 2 tablespoons parsley
- 2 tablespoons cheese, grated
- A pinch chili powder
- Black pepper and salt, to taste
- Cooking spray, as needed

How to make it:

1. Place your instant pot on a dry surface.
2. Open the lid; grease inside cooking surface with cooking spray.
3. In a medium bowl, thoroughly whisk the eggs.
4. Add the remaining ingredients except for the cheese. Season with black pepper and salt.
5. Add the mixture to the instant pot.
6. Close the lid and make sure it is sealed properly.
7. Press STEAM; set timer to 5 minutes.
8. The instant pot will start building pressure; allow the mixture to cook for the set time.
9. After the timer reaches zero, turn venting knob from sealing to the venting position. Wait until float valve drops (1-2 minutes).
10. Open the lid and transfer the food to a plate.
11. Top with the cheese; slice in half and serve warm.

Jar Breakfast:

Serves: 2
Preparation Time: 15 minutes
Cooking Time: 5 minutes
Macros per serving:

Calories: 632
Protein: 38 grams
Fat: 46 grams
Carbohydrates: 16 grams

Ingredients:

- 4 eggs
- 4 pieces bacon, cooked of your preferred breakfast meat, such as sausage
- 4 tablespoons peach-mango salsa, divided
- 6 slices sharp cheese or shredded, cheese, Divided
- Tater tots

Equipment:

- 2 pieces mason jars (that can hold about 2-cup worth ingredients)

How to make it:

1. Put 1¼ cups water in the inner pot. Put enough tater tots cover the bottom of the mason jars. Crock 2 eggs in each. Poke the yolks using a fork or tip of a long thin knife. Add your choice of meats, 2 slices cheese to cover the ingredients, and 2 tablespoons salsa. Add more tater tots and top with 1 slice cheese. Tightly cover the jars with foil. Put the jars in the IP, right in the water.
2. Lock the lid and close the pressure valve. Set the IP to MANUAL high pressure for 5 minutes. QPR when the timer beeps. Open the lid. Carefully remove the jars. Serve.

Vanilla Peach Oats:

Serves: 2
Preparation Time: 5 minutes
Cooking Time: 3 minutes
Macros per serving:

Calories: 193
Protein: 6.3 grams
Fat: 3.3 grams
Carbohydrates: 27.6 grams

Ingredients:

- 1 peach, chopped
- 2 cups of water
- 1 cups rolled oats
- ½ teaspoon vanilla
- 1 tablespoon flax meal
- ½ tablespoon maple syrup

How to make it:

1. Place everything in your instant pot. Stir to combine well.
2. Close the lid, and turn the vents to "sealed"
3. Press "Pressure Cook" (manual) button, use "+" or "-"button to set the timer for 3 minutes. Use "pressure level" button to set the pressure to high.
4. Once the timer is up, press the "cancel" button and allow the pressure to be released naturally until the float valve drops down.
5. Open the lid. Serve and enjoy!

Pecan Pie Oatmeal:

Serves: 2
Preparation Time: 5 minutes
Cooking Time: 3 minutes
Macros per serving:

Calories: 230
Protein: 4 grams
Fat: 8.2 grams
Carbohydrates: 37.1 grams

Ingredients:

- ½ cup steel cut oats
- 1¾ cups water
- 1/8 cup half & half
- 2 Medjool dates, Chopped
- ¼ cup pecans, chopped
- 3 tablespoons maple syrup
- ½ teaspoon ground cinnamon
- ¼ teaspoon nutmeg

How to make it:

1. Add all of the ingredients to your instant pot and stir.
2. Close the lid and cook at high for three minutes.
3. When the cooking is complete, does a natural pressure release.
4. Serve warm with maple syrup.

Berry Chia Oats:

Serves: 2
Preparation Time: 5 minutes
Cooking Time: 6 minutes

Macros per serving:

Calories: 114
Protein: 4.5 grams
Fat: 3 grams
Carbohydrates: 18 grams

Ingredients:

- 1/2 cups old fashioned oats
- ½ cups almond milk, unsweetened
- ½ cups blueberries
- 1 teaspoon chia seeds
- Sweetener or sugar as needed
- Splash of vanilla
- Pinch of salt
- A pinch ground cinnamon
- 1 ½ cups water

How to make it:

1. In the medium bowl, thoroughly mix all the ingredients, add the bowl mixture to a pint-size jar and cover with an aluminum foil.
2. In the pot, slowly pour the water. Take the trivet and arrange inside it; place the jar over it.
3. Close the lid and lock. Ensure that you have sealed the valve to avoid leakage.
4. Press "Manual" mode and set the timer for six minutes. It will take a few minutes for the pot to build inside pressure and start cooking.
5. After the timer reads zero, press "cancel" and naturally release pressure. It takes about 8-10 minutes to release pressure naturally.
6. Carefully remove the lid and take out the jar. Mix in the oatmeal; serve warm!

Potato Ham Breakfast Casserole:

Serves: 2
Preparation Time: 5 minutes
Cooking Time: 16 minutes
Macros per serving:

Calories: 528
Protein: 13.6 grams
Fat: 27.3 grams
Carbohydrates: 46.8 grams

Ingredients:

- 1 stick butter
- ¼ cup milk
- ¼ cup sour cream
- ¾ pound potatoes, diced and cooked
- ¾ cup mixed cheese, shredded
- ¼ cup ham, diced
- 2 green onion, sliced
- Black pepper and salt, as needed

How to make it:

1. Place your instant pot on a dry surface and open the lid.
2. Press SAUTE; add the butter and melt it.
3. Mix in the onions and potato; cook; for 4 minutes until soft and translucent.
4. Add the milk, ham, sour cream, a pinch black pepper (ground) and salt; stir them well to coat.
5. Add the cheese on top.
6. Close the lid and make sure it is sealed properly.
7. Press MANUAL; set timer to 12 minutes.
8. The instant pot will start building pressure; allow the mixture to cook for the set time.
9. After the timer reaches zero, wait for the float valve to drop. It will take 8-10 minutes.
10. Open the lid and transfer the food to a plate.
11. Divide among serving plates/bowls; serve warm.

Boiled Eggs:

Serves: 2
Preparation Time: 5 minutes
Cooking Time: 3-9 minutes

Macros per serving:

Calories: 63
Protein: 5.5 grams
Fat: 4.4 grams
Carbohydrates: 0.3 grams

Ingredients:

- Large eggs, as much as you need
- 1 cup of water

How to make it:

1. Put the IP steamer basket and pour 1 cup water in the inner pot. Put the eggs in the steamer. Lock the lid and close the pressure valve. Set the IP to low PRESSURE for 3-4 minutes for soft boiled, 5-7 minutes for medium-boiled, or 8-9 minutes for hard-boiled eggs.
2. Ready a bowl and half fill it with cold water and ice. QPR when the timer beeps. Open the lid. Transfer the eggs immediately in the ice bath. Let cool for 5 to 10 minutes .serve.

Ham Sausage Quiche:

Serves: 2
Preparation Time: 5 minutes
Cooking Time: 30 minutes
Macros per serving:

Calories: 396
Protein: 28.6 grams
Fat: 31.7 grams
Carbohydrates: 4.3 grams

Ingredients:

- 1 cups of water
- 3 eggs
- 2 bacon slices, cooked and crumbled
- ¼ cup milk
- 1/4 cup diced ham
- ½ cup cooked ground sausage
- ½ pinch of black pepper
- ½ cup grated cheddar cheese
- 1 bunch of green onions, chopped
- 1 scallion, chopped

How to make it:

1. Pour the water into your instant pot. Whisk the eggs along with the salt, pepper, and milk, in a bowl.
2. In a 1-quart baking dish, add the bacon, sausage, ham, and mix to combine.
3. Pour the eggs over, and stir to combine again
4. Sprinkle with green onions and cheese.
5. Cover with foil and place in the instant pot.
6. Close the lid, and switch the vent to "sealed".
7. Press "pressure cook" (manual) button, use "+" or "-"button to set the timer for 30 minutes. Use "pressure level" button to set the pressure to high.
8. Once the timer is up press "cancel" button and turns the steam release handle to "venting" position for quick release until the float valve drops down.
9. Open the lid. Serve warm.

Millet Porridge:

Serves: 2
Preparation Time: 10 minutes
Cooking Time: 9 minutes
Macros per serving:

Calories: 245
Protein: 5.7 grams
Fat: 2.2 grams
Carbohydrates: 51.4 grams

Ingredients:

- 1 cup of water
- ½ cup millet
- 1 ½ tablespoon honey
- 3 tablespoons fresh blueberries

How to make it:

1. In the instant pot, mix together water and millet.
2. Secure the lid and cook at air mass for ten minutes.
3. After the cooking is complete, use a quick pressure release.
4. Remove the lid and with a fork. Fluff the porridge.
5. Drizzle with honey and serve with a topping of blueberries.

Chia Spiced Rice Pudding:

Serves: 2
Preparation Time: 5 minutes
Cooking Time: 15 minutes
Macros per serving:

Calories: 242
Protein: 2.5 grams
Fat: 2 grams
Carbohydrates: 31.5 grams

Ingredients:

- 6 Medjool dates, sliced
- 2 tablespoons brown sugar
- 1 teaspoon cinnamon powder
- 1 cup short-grain rice
- 1 teaspoon ginger powder
- 1 cup almond milk, unsweetened
- 1½ cups water
- 1 cup coconut milk, unsweetened
- ¼ teaspoon nutmeg
- 5 cardamom pods
- 1 teaspoon vanilla extract
- Pinch of salt

How to make it:

1. Take your instant pot and place it on a clean kitchen platform. Turn it on after plugging it into a power socket.
2. Open the lid from the top and put it aside; start adding the mentioned ingredients inside and gently stir them. Do not add the garnishes.
3. Close the lid and lock. Ensure that you have sealed the valve to avoid leakage.
4. Press "Manual" mode and set a timer for 10 minutes. It will take a few minutes for the pot to build inside pressure and start cooking.
5. After the timer reads zero, press "cancel" and naturally release pressure. It takes about 8-10 minutes to naturally release pressure.
6. Carefully remove the lid and mix the rice. Top with the garnishes and serve warm!

Cheesy Bacon Oats:

Serves: 2
Preparation Time: 5 minutes
Cooking Time: 12 minutes
Macros per serving:

Calories: 287
Protein: 11.3 grams
Fat: 23.2 grams
Carbohydrates: 21 grams

Ingredients:

- 4 slices bacon, cooked and crumbled
- 1 small onion, finely chopped
- ¼ cup Gouda cheese, shredded
- ¼ cup of water
- 6 ounces chicken stock
- ½ cup steel-cut oats
- 1 tablespoon butter
- 1 tablespoon olive oil
- Black pepper and salt, as needed

How to make it:

1. Place your instant pot on a dry surface and open the lid.
2. Press SAUTE; add the butter and melt it.
3. Mix in the onion; cook for 3 minutes until soft and translucent.
4. Add the oats, stock, olive oil, a pinch of black pepper (ground) and salt.
5. Close the lid and make sure it is sealed properly.
6. Press MANUAL; set timer to 9 minutes.
7. The instant pot will start building pressure; allow the mixture to cook for the set time.
8. After the timer reaches zero, wait for the float valve to drop. It will take 8-10 minutes.
9. Open the lid and transfer the food to a plate.
10. Divide among serving plates/bowls; serve warm.

Crunchy Cinnamon Toast Rice Pudding:

Serves: 2
Preparation Time: 10 minutes
Cooking Time: 25 minutes
Macros per serving:

Calories: 420
Protein: 10 grams
Fat: 7 grams
Carbohydrates: 78 grams

Ingredients:

- 1 cup of water
- 1/8 teaspoon ground cinnamon, plus extra for topping
- ¼ cup of sugar
- 1/3 teaspoon vanilla extract
- ¾ cup Arborio rice
- 1 1/3 tablespoon maple syrup
- 1 ½ egg
- 1 1/3 cups whole milk, divided into 1 cups and 1/3 cup
- 1 bay leaf
- 2 dashes ground nutmeg
- Cinnamon toast crunch cereal, for topping
- About 1 tablespoon eggnog, for serving, optional

How to make it:

1. Put the rice salt, bay leaf, and water in the inner pot. Lock the lid and close the pressure valve. Set the IP to MANUAL high pressure for 3 minutes. NPR for 10 minutes when the timer beeps, then QPR. While the rice is cooking, put the eggs, 1/3 cup milk, vanilla, cinnamon, and nutmeg in a mixing bowl. Whisk until combined well. Set aside. Open the IP lid. Remove and discard bay leaf.
2. Add the 1 cup milk, maple syrup, and sugar; stir to combine well, scraping the bottom of the pot to dislodge stuck rice. Set a fine-mesh strainer on the IP lid.
3. Pour the custard mixture through a strainer. Immediately press the CANCEL key. Set the IP to SAUTE "more" mode. Stir constantly for 3 to 5 minutes until the mixture is bubbly and sticky. Turn the IP off. Immediately remove the inner pot from the housing and put on a heat-safe surface. This step should take 5 minutes tops. You can eat the pudding while warm. If you want it cold, let the inner pot cool. Cover and refrigerate the pudding for at least 2 to 3 hours. Serve topped with the cereal. If you want to thin the mixture, add heavy cream, half-and-half, milk, or eggnog to your serving before topping.

Bacon Egg Mystery Muffins:

Serves: 2
Preparation Time: 5 minutes
Cooking Time: 10 minutes

Macros per serving:

Calories: 72
Protein: 4.3 grams
Fat: 2.6 grams
Carbohydrates: 1.6 grams

Ingredients:

- 1 cups of water
- 2 bacon slices, cooked and crumbled, divided
- 1/8 teaspoon lemon pepper seasoning
- 2 eggs
- ½ scallion, chopped and divided
- 2 tablespoon shredded cheddar cheese, divided
- Salt to taste

How to make it:

1. In a bowl, whisk together the eggs, lemon pepper, and salt
2. Divide the cheese onion and bacon, between 2 silicone muffin cups.
3. Pour the egg mixture over.
4. Pour the water into your instant pot and arrange the muffin cups on the rack.
5. Close the lid, and turn the vent to: sealed"
6. Press "pressure cook" (manual) button, use "+" or "-"button to set the timer for 10 minutes. Use "pressure level" button to set the pressure to high.
7. Once the timer is up press "Cancel" button and turns the steam release handle to "venting" position for quick release until the float valve drops down.
8. Open the lid. Serve and enjoy!

Chicken Recipes

Barbecue Chicken:

Serves: 2
Preparation Time: 5 minutes
Cooking Time: 15 minutes
Macros per serving:

Calories: 128
Protein: 14.1 grams
Fat: 1.9 grams
Carbohydrates: 12.9 grams

Ingredients:

- 2 chicken breasts split in half
- 1 cup chicken stock
- ½ cup of water
- 1 teaspoon nutmeg
- 1 teaspoon cinnamon
- 1 teaspoon ginger
- ¼ teaspoon salt
- 1 teaspoon pepper
- ½ cup barbecue sauce (use your favorite)

How to make it:

1. Combine the salt, pepper, ginger, cinnamon, and nutmeg in a small bowl and rub the mixture into the chicken breasts.
2. Place chicken in the instant pot and cover with the water and the chicken stock.
3. Close the lid and cook at air mass for quarter-hour.
4. When the cooking is complete, does a quick pressure release.
5. Remove the chicken and cover with barbecue sauce.

Tangy Cranberry Turkey:

Serves: 2
Preparation Time: 8-10 minutes
Cooking Time: 20 minutes

Macros per serving:

Calories: 236
Protein: 15 grams
Fat: 4 grams
Carbohydrates: 6 grams

Ingredients:

- 2 tablespoons olive oil
- 1 ½ cups cranberries, dried
- 1 yellow onion, roughly chopped
- 1 cup of orange juice
- 1 cup walnuts
- 4 turkey wings
- 2 tablespoons ghee, melted
- A pinch of pepper and salt
- 1 bunch thyme, chopped

How to make it:

- Switch on your instant pot after placing it on a clean and dry kitchen platform. Press "sauté" cooking function.
- Open the pot lid; add the oil, ghee, turkey, pepper, and salt in the pot; start cooking to brown evenly. Transfer to a plate.
- Add the onion, Walnuts, berries, and thyme to the pot; stir and cook for 2-3 minutes.
- Mix the orange juice, return turkey wings to pot, stir gently.
- Close the pot by closing the top lid. Also, ensure to seal the valve.
- Press "manual" cooking function and set the cooking time to 20 minutes. It will start cooking after a few minutes. Let the pot mix cook under pressure until the timer reads zero.
- Turn off and press "cancel" cooking function. Quick-release pressure.
- Open the pot. Divider turkey wings between plates and keep warm.
- Set instant pot on simmer mode, cook cranberry mix for 4-5 minutes more. Drizzle the mix over turkey wings and serve warm!

Sweet Chicken Retreat:

Serves: 2
Preparation Time: 5 minutes
Cooking Time: 15 minutes
Macros per serving:

Calories: 465
Protein: 31 grams
Fat: 22.7 grams
Carbohydrates: 15.3 grams

Ingredients:

- 2 bay leaves
- ¼ cup chopped onion
- 4 tablespoons apple cider vinegar
- 1 pound chicken wings
- ½ teaspoon salt
- 2 teaspoons black pepper
- 6-7 tablespoons low-sodium soy sauce
- ¼ cup of sugar

How to make it:

1. Place your instant pot on a dry surface.
2. Open the lid, add the listed ingredients, and stir to combine using a wooden spatula.
3. Close the lid and make sure it is sealed properly.
4. Press MANUAL; set timer to 15 minutes.
5. The instant pot will start building pressure; allow the mixture to cook for the set time.
6. After the timer reaches zero, wait for the float valve to drop. It will take 8-10 minutes.
7. Open the lid and transfer the food to a plate.
8. Divide among serving plates/bowls; serve warm.

Creamy Chicken with Mushroom:

Serves: 2
Preparation Time: 15 minutes
Cooking Time: 20 minutes
Macros per serving:

Calories: 713
Protein: 73 grams
Fat: 41 grams
Carbohydrates: 15 grams

Ingredients:

- 1 will coconut milk, chilled nightlong within the refrigerator
- 1 pounds chicken thighs
- 1 tablespoon water
- 1 teaspoon dried thyme
- 1 teaspoon garlic powder
- 1 teaspoon onion powder
- 1 teaspoon salt
- 2 tablespoons tapioca starch
- 8 ounces baby portabella mushrooms, sliced
- Chicken broth, enough to fill the can of coconut
- Cream after the coconut water is poured out

How to make it:

1. Turn the can of coconut milk upside down without shaking it. Open the can. The coconut water and cream should be separated with the coconut water on top.
2. Pour out or scoop the coconut water from the can. Add broth into the can, filling it to the top. Pour the broth and coconut cream into a medium bowl. Add the spices to the bowl. Whisk until combine well.
3. Put the chicken in the inner pot. Put the mushrooms on the chicken, covering the meat. Pour the coconut cream mixture over the mushrooms and chicken. Lock the lid and close the pressure valve. Set the IP to MANUAL high pressure for 8 to 10 minutes. NPR completely when the timer beeps. Open the lid.
4. Using a slotted spoon, transfer the chicken and mushroom to a serving platter. Leave the cooking liquid in the pot. Discard ½ of the cooking liquid. Set the IP to SAUTE. Whisk the water and starch in a small bowl until smooth. When the cooking liquid is boiling, whisk in the starch mixture until it is gravy thick. Turn the IP off. Ladle the gravy over the chicken. Serve.

Noodle Cream Chicken:

Serves: 2
Preparation Time: 5 minutes
Cooking Time: 30 minutes

Macros per serving:

Calories: 260
Protein: 16.3 grams
Fat: 29 grams
Carbohydrates: 5.9 grams

Ingredients:

- 1 tablespoon oil
- 2 chicken leg quarters, bone-in
- 1 small onion, well diced
- 1 teaspoon salt
- 1 cup chicken broth
- 2 teaspoons hot paprika
- ½ cup sour cream
- 1 medium tomato, skin removed & coarsely chopped

How to make it:

1. Add oil to instant pot and press "sauté" button ("normal" preset), wait till you see hot on the display.
2. Add chicken and brown it for 4-5 minutes until golden brown. Add broth, onions, and paprika to the instant pot.
3. Put tomatoes on top of the chicken, and sprinkle it with salt. Make sure NOT to stir.
4. Close the lid, and switch the vent to "sealed".
5. Press "Pressure Cook" (manual) button, use "+" or "-"button to set the timer for 10 minutes.
6. Use "pressure level" button to set the pressure to high. Once the timer is up, press the "cancel" button and allow the pressure to be released naturally until the float valve drops down. Open the lid.
7. Take out chicken from instant pot and let it cool. Press the "sauté" button and adjust to "less" preset, sauté for 15 minutes until the leftover liquid thickens.
8. Take ¼ cup cooking juice out of the instant pot and add to the sour cream and stir evenly mixed.
9. Put the cream mixture and chicken back into the instant pot and simmer for a few minutes.
10. Serve chicken with sauce on top with noodles on the side.

Pina Colada Chicken:

Serves: 2
Preparation Time: 10 minutes
Cooking Time: 15 minutes
Macros per serving:

Calories: 572
Protein: 66.9 grams
Fat: 26.1 grams
Carbohydrates: 14.9 grams

Ingredients:

- 2 pounds boned chicken thighs, delve tiny items
- 1 cup pineapple, diced
- ½ cup coconut cream
- ½ teaspoon salt
- 1 teaspoon ground cinnamon
- ¾ cup green onions, chopped
- 2 tablespoons desiccated coconut shavings
- 1 tablespoon arrowroot powder
- 1 tablespoon water

How to make it:

1. Add all the ingredients to the instant pot, except for the green onions, and mix well.
2. Press the POULTRY button and cook at high pressure for 15 minutes.
3. When the cooking is complete, do a quick pressure release.
4. Add the arrowroot powder to a tablespoon of water, mix, and add it to the chicken. Let it simmer for some minutes till it thickens.
5. Garnish with chopped green onions and serve.

Oregano Pasta Chicken:

Serves: 2
Preparation Time: 5 minutes
Cooking Time: 15 minutes
Macros per serving:

Calories: 102
Protein: 15.5 grams
Fat: 2.5 grams
Carbohydrates: 4 grams

Ingredients:

- ½ teaspoon olive oil
- ½ cup diced tomatoes
- ½ cup diced red bell pepper
- ½ teaspoon oregano
- 1 bay leaf
- ½ cup chopped onion
- 1 ½ cup diced chicken
- ¼ teaspoon salt
- ½ teaspoon pepper
- 2 tablespoons chopped parsley
- Cooked pasta of your choice

How to make it:

1. Switch on the pot after placing it on a clean and dry platform. Press "sauté" cooking function.
2. Open the pot lid; add the oil and onions in the pot; cook for 2 minutes to cook well and soften.
3. Add the chicken, bell pepper, and diced tomatoes. Mix the salt, pepper, oregano, and bay leaf.
4. Close the pot by closing the top lid. Also, ensure to seal the valve.
5. Press "Manual" cooking function and set the cooking time to 10 minutes. It will start cooking after a few minutes. Let the pot mix cook under pressure until the timer reads zero.
6. Press "cancel" preparation performs and press "natural unharness (NPR)" setting. It will take 8-10 minutes for natural pressure release.
7. Open the pot; top with some parsley and serve with cooked pasta!

Sweet BBQ Chicken Wings:

Serves: 2
Preparation Time: 5 minutes
Cooking Time: 12-15 minutes
Macros per serving:

Calories: 513
Protein: 39.7 grams
Fat: 28.7 grams
Carbohydrates: 18.2 grams

Ingredients:

- 1 ½ tablespoon raw honey
- 1 pound chicken wings
- ¼ cup barbecue sauce
- 1/8 teaspoon salt
- ½ cup of water
- ¼ cup chopped onion
- ¼ teaspoon pepper

How to make it:

1. Place your instant pot on a dry surface.
2. Open the lid, add the listed ingredients, and stir to combine using a wooden spatula.
3. Close the lid and make sure it is sealed properly.
4. Press MANUAL; set timer to 10 minutes.
5. The instant pot will start building pressure; allow the mixture to cook for the set time.
6. After the timer reaches zero, turn venting knob from sealing to the venting position. Wait until float valve drops (1-2 minutes).
7. Open the pot and transfer the mixture to a saucepan.
8. Cook for a few minutes to thicken the liquid.
9. Serve warm.

Turkey Legs with Gravy:

Serves: 2
Preparation Time: 10 minutes
Cooking Time: 30 minutes
Macros per serving:

Calories: 295
Protein: 35 grams
Fat: 13 grams
Carbohydrates: 8 grams

Ingredients:

- 1 cup chicken stock, homemade, unsalted
- 1 dash sherry wine
- 1 onion, small-sized, sliced
- 1 pinch rosemary
- 1 pinch thyme
- 1 stalk celery, chopped
- 1 tablespoon light soy sauce
- 1 tablespoon olive oil
- 2 bay leaves
- 2 pieces of turkey legs
- 3 cloves garlic, roughly minced
- Kosher salt and ground black pepper, to taste

How to make it:

1. Generously season the turkey with pepper and salt. Set the IP to Sauté "more" mode. When hot, put the oil in the inner pot, spreading it to coat the bottom. Add the turkey. Cook each side for 2 to 3 minutes or until brown. Transfer to a plate. Set aside until using.
2. Press the CANCEL key. Set the IP to SAUTE "normal" mode. Add the onion. Season with 1 pinch pepper and salt. Cook for (one) 1 minute or until soft. Add the garlic. Sauté for 30 seconds or until fragrant. Add the celery. Sauté for (one) 1 minute. Season with 1 pinch pepper and salt if desired. Add the bay leaves. Slightly scrunch the rosemary and thyme. Add to the pot. Stir to mix. Add the wine to deglaze, scraping the browned bits off the pot. Cook until the alcohol has evaporated. Add the stock and soy sauce. Stir to mix. Season with pepper and salt as needed. Press the CANCEL key.
3. Lock the lid and close the pressure valve. Set the IP to MANUAL high pressure for 18 to 20 minutes. NPR for 10 minutes when the timer beeps, then QPR. Open the lid. Transfer the turkey to a plate using tongs. Set the IP to SAUTE. Mix the water and cornstarch in a small bowl until smooth. Pour in the pot. Stir until thick.

Rosemary Wine Chicken:

Serves: 2-3
Preparation Time: 5 minutes
Cooking Time: 15 minutes
Macros per serving:

Calories: 192
Protein: 14.4 grams
Fat: 27.7 grams
Carbohydrates: 1.9 grams

Ingredients:

- 3 chicken breast halves, boneless and skinless
- 1 teaspoon rosemary
- 2 garlic cloves, peeled and sliced
- ¼ cup parsley, chopped
- 1 cup chicken broth
- ½ cup white wine
- 2 tablespoon olive oil
- Salt and pepper, to taste
- ½ lemon, thinly sliced

How to make it:

1. Add oil to instant pot and press "sauté" button ("normal" preset), wait till you see hot on the display.
2. Add chicken breasts, cook for 6-7 minutes both sides with the lid open until all sides are browned. Season the chicken with rosemary and add garlic.
3. Press "cancel" button. Mix wine, broth, and parsley in a bowl. Add the mixture to the pot.
4. Close the lid, and switch the vent to "Sealed".
5. Press "pressure cook" (manual) button, use "+" or "–" button to set the timer for 8 minutes. Use "pressure level" button to set the pressure to high.
6. Once the time is an up press "cancel" button and turns the steamer release handle to "venting" position for quick release, until the float valve drops down.
7. Open the lid.
8. Put lemon slices on top before serving.

Cacciatore Chicken:

Serves: 2
Preparation Time: 5 minutes
Cooking Time: 15 minutes
Macros per serving:

Calories: 327
Protein: 27.3 grams
Fat: 18.5 grams
Carbohydrates: 13.2 grams

Ingredients:

- 6 chicken thighs
- 1 large yellow onion, chopped
- 1 cup chicken broth
- 1 bay leaf
- 1 teaspoon garlic powder
- 1 teaspoon oregano
- ¾ cup black olives
- ¼ teaspoon salt
- 6 medium tomatoes, chopped

How to make it:

1. Add all the ingredients to the instant pot, except olives.
2. Close the lid and cook at air mass for quarter-hour.
3. When the cooking is complete, do a natural pressure release.
4. Garnish with olives and serve.

Oregano Pasta Chicken:

Serves: 2
Preparation Time: 5 minutes
Cooking Time: 15 minutes
Macros per serving:

Calories: 102
Protein: 15.5 grams
Fat: 2.5 grams
Carbohydrates: 4 grams

Ingredients:

- ½ teaspoon olive oil
- ½ cup diced tomatoes
- ½ cup diced red bell pepper
- ½ teaspoon oregano
- 1 bay leaf
- ½ cup chopped onion
- 1 ½ cup diced chicken
- ¼ teaspoon salt
- ½ teaspoon pepper
- 2 tablespoons chopped parsley
- Cooked pasta of your choice

How to make it:

1. Switch on the pot after placing it on a clean and dry platform. Press "sauté" cooking function.
2. Open the pot lid; add the oil and onions in the pot; cook for 2 minutes to cook well and soften.
3. Add the chicken, bell pepper, and diced tomatoes. Mix the salt, pepper, oregano, and bay leaf.
4. Close the pot by closing the top lid. Also, ensure to seal the valve.
5. Press "Manual" cooking function and set the cooking time to 10 minutes. It will start cooking after a few minutes. Let the pot mix cook under pressure until the time reads zero.
6. Press "Cancel" change of state operates and press "Natural unharness (NPR)" setting. It will take 8-10 minutes for natural pressure release.
7. Open the pot; top with some parsley and serve with cooked pasts!

Chicken Olives Feast:

Serves: 2
Preparation Time: 5 minutes
Cooking Time: 35 minutes
Macros per serving:

Calories: 248
Protein: 15 grams
Fat: 16.2 grams
Carbohydrates: 13.4 grams

Ingredients:

- 1 small yellow onion, diced
- ¼ cup kalamata olives pitted
- 1 small red bell pepper, sliced
- 4 ounces tomato, crushed
- 2 chicken thighs, skinless
- 2 baby carrots, sliced
- 1 tablespoon olive oil
- ½ teaspoon dry oregano
- Black pepper and salt, to taste

How to make it:

1. Place your instant pot on a dry surface and open the lid.
2. Press SAUTE; add the oil and heat it.
3. Add and cook the chicken thighs for 3 minutes on each side to evenly brown.
4. Drain the chicken thighs and set them aside in a container.
5. Add the onion, bell pepper and carrot to the instant pot and cook them for 4 minutes.
6. Return the chicken, along with the tomato, oregano, a pinch black pepper (ground) and salt.
7. Close the lid and make sure it is sealed properly.
8. Press MANUAL; set timer to 25 minutes.
9. The instant pot will start building pressure; allow the mixture to cook for the set time.
10. After the timer reaches zero, wait for the float valve to drop. It will take 8-10 minutes.
11. Open the lid and transfer the food to a plate.
12. Divide among serving plates/bowls; serve warm.

Braised Chicken with Parsley and Capers:

Serves: 2
Preparation Time: 15 minutes
Cooking Time: 25 minutes
Macros per serving:

Calories: 276
Protein: 36 grams
Fat: 11 grams
Carbohydrates: 6 grams

Ingredients:

- 7 ¼ ounces could chicken broth
- 2 chicken breast, skinless, bone-in
- 1/6 cup white wine vinegar
- 1/6 cup salted capers, soaked well in several changes of water
- ¼ cup Petroselinum crispum neapolitanum, minced, plus more for garnish
- ½ tablespoon cornstarch
- ½ onions, large-sized, minced
- 1 tablespoon olive oil, divided
- Freshly ground black pepper
- Salt

How to make it:

1. Generously season the chicken with pepper and salt. Set the IP to SAUTE. Put ½ tablespoon oil in the inner pot. When the oil is hot, add the chicken. Cook until both sides are brown. Transfer to a plate. Put the remaining oil in the pot. When hot, add the onion. Cook for 5 minutes or until soft, stirring constantly. Add the parsley and capers. Cook for (one) 1 minute. Add the broth. Stir. Add the vinegar. Stir. Add the cooked chicken, along with juices accumulated on the plate. Lock the lid and close the pressure valve. Set the scientific discipline to MANUAL high for thirteen minutes. QPR when the timer beeps.
2. Open the lid. Transfer the chicken to a platter using tongs. Tent with foil to keep warm. Mix the water and cornflour in a very little bowl. Set the IP to SAUTE. Bring the broth to boil. Add the cornstarch mix, stirring constantly until the sauce is thick. Turn the IP off. Season with pepper and salt as needed. Spoon the sauce over the chicken. Serve garnished with parsley.

Chicken Parmesan Risotto:

Serves: 2
Preparation Time: 5 minutes
Cooking Time: 15 minutes
Macros per serving:

Calories: 586
Protein: 45 grams
Fat: 22.5 grams
Carbohydrates: 23.6 grams

Ingredients:

- ¾ lb. chicken meat, diced
- 2-3 slices pancetta, diced
- ¾ cup risotto or Arborio rice
- ½ onion, chopped
- 2 garlic cloves, chopped
- 1 tablespoon unsalted butter
- 1 tablespoon olive oil
- 2 tablespoon parmesan, grated
- 1/3 cup white wine
- 3 ½ cups chicken stock
- 1 teaspoon fresh thyme
- 1 tablespoon lemon zest
- Salt, pepper, to taste

How to make it:

1. Add oil and butter to instant pot and press "SAUTE" button ("normal" preset), wait till you see hot on the display.
2. Add onion, cook for 1-2 minutes. Add pancetta, chicken, and garlic. Cook for another 2-3 minutes.
3. Add rice mix well, the rice should be covered with oil-butter mixture. Add wine and scrape the sides of the pot.
4. Cook for 2-3 minutes stirring constantly. Press "Cancel" button. Add chicken stock, thyme, lemon zest, salt, and pepper.
5. Close the lid, and switch the vent to "SEALED".
6. Press "pressure cook" (Manual) button, use "+" or "-"button to set the timer for 6 minutes. Use "pressure level" button to set the pressure to high.
7. Once the timer is up, press the "Cancel" button and allow the pressure to be released naturally until the float valve drops down. Open the lid.
8. Add parmesan cheese to the pot and stir until it melts. Serve topped with extra parmesan and lemon zest.

Beef, Pork & Lamb Recipes

Beef Bourguignon:

Serves: 2
Preparation Time: 10 minutes
Cooking Time: 50 minutes
Macros per serving:

Calories: 559
Protein: 43.3 grams
Fat: 17 grams
Carbohydrates: 47.5 grams

Ingredients:

- ½ pound beef stew meat
- 2 bacon slices
- 1 garlic clove, minced
- 1 medium onion, chopped
- 2 medium carrots, chopped
- 1 tablespoon parsley
- 1 tablespoon thyme
- ½ cup beef stock
- ½ cup red wine
- 1 large potato, cubed
- ½ tablespoon honey
- ½ tablespoon olive oil

How to make it:

1. Place the oil within the instant pot and choose SAUTE. Add beef and cook for 3-4 minutes or until browned. Set the beef aside.
2. Add bacon and onion, and sauté until onion is translucent.
3. Add beef and the rest of the ingredient and close the lid
4. Cook at high pressure for 30 minutes.
5. When the cooking is complete, do a natural pressure release.
6. Serve warm.

Artichoke Mayo Beef:

Serves: 2
Preparation Time: 10 minutes
Cooking Time: 15 minutes
Macros per serving:

Calories: 544
Protein: 41 grams
Fat: 19 grams
Carbohydrates: 48.5 grams

Ingredients:

- 1 pound beef, ground
- 1 small yellow onion, chopped
- ½ teaspoon dill, dried
- ½ teaspoon apple cider vinegar
- 3 tablespoons mayonnaise
- ½ teaspoon garlic powder
- ½ teaspoon oregano, dried
- ½ tablespoon olive oil
- 1/3 cup water
- ½ teaspoon onion powder
- A pinch of pepper and salt
- 1 ¼ cup artichoke hearts

How to make it:

1. Take your 3-quart instant pot; open the top lid. Plug it and turn it on.
2. Press "SAUTE" setting and the pot will start heating up.
3. In the cooking pot area, add the oil and onions. Cook until starts becoming translucent and softened for 3 minutes. Stir in between.
4. Add the beef, salt, pepper, oregano, doll, garlic, and onion powder, stir and cook for 3 minutes.
5. Add water and artichokes; stir gently.
6. Close the top lid and seal its valve.
7. Press the "MANUAL" setting. Adjust cooking time to 7 minutes.
8. Allow the recipe to cook for the set cooking time.
9. After the set cooking time ends, press "CANCEL" and then press "QPR (Quick Pressure Release)."
10. Instant pot will quickly release the pressure.
11. Open the top lid; add the cooked recipe mix is serving plates.
12. Drain excess water, mix the vinegar and mayo.
13. Serve and enjoy!

Balsamic Soy Beef Roast:

Serves: 2
Preparation Time: 5 minutes
Cooking Time: 30 minutes
Macros per serving:

Calories: 248
Protein: 36.2 grams
Fat: 9 grams
Carbohydrates: 8.3 grams

Ingredients:

- 2 tablespoons balsamic vinegar
- 1 teaspoon soy sauce
- 1 pound beef roast
- ¼ cup beef stock
- 1 clove garlic, minced
- 1 teaspoon Worcestershire sauce
- Black pepper and salt, to taste
- Cooking spray, as needed

How to make it:

1. Season the roast with some black pepper (ground) and salt.
2. Place your instant pot on a dry surface.
3. Open the lid; grease inside cooking surface with cooking spray.
4. Add the roast and other ingredients and stir to combine using a wooden spatula.
5. Close the lid and certify it's sealed properly.
6. Press MANUAL; set timer to 30 minutes.
7. The instant pot will start building pressure; allow the mixture to cook for the set time.
8. After the timer reaches zero, turn venting knob from sealing to the venting position. Wait until float valve drops (1-2 minutes).
9. Open the lid and transfer the food to a plate.
10. Divide among serving plates/bowls; serve warm.

Corned Beef with Cabbage:

Serves: 2
Preparation Time: 5 minutes
Cooking Time: 1 hour 35 minutes
Macros per serving:

Calories: 820
Protein: 60 grams
Fat: 60 grams
Carbohydrates: 9 grams

Ingredients:

- 1 pound corned beef brisket with spices
- 1 cup baby carrots
- ½ small head green cabbage, sliced into 4 wedges
- 2 ½ cups water, or more as needed

How to make it:

1. If suing cured corned beef, drain and rinse. If using uncured, leave as is.
2. Put the corned beef in the IP along with the spices. Pour the water into the pot, adding more as need until the water level is even with the top of the corned beef. Push and flatten the beef down as needed.
3. Lock the lid and close the pressure valve. Set the IP to MANUAL high pressure for 90 minutes. QPR when the timer beeps. The beef is done if a fork pierces easily through the thickest part of the meat.
4. It the fork meets resistance, cook for 10 minutes more at MANUAL high pressure. Without removing the beef from the pot, add the cabbage and carrots around the meat. Do not fill the inner pot past the maximum capacity.
5. Lock the lid and close the pressure valve. Set the IP to MANUAL high pressure for 5 minutes. QPR when the timer beeps.
6. Remove your beef and veggies from the pot. Slice the meat into thick pieces, going against the grain. Serve with the carrots and cabbages.

Mozzarella Beef Lasagna:

Serves: 2
Preparation Time: 5 minutes
Cooking Time: 40 minutes
Macros per serving:

Calories: 712
Protein: 56.7 grams
Fat: 19.1 grams
Carbohydrates: 35.1 grams

Ingredients:

- ½ pound ground beef
- 6 uncooked lasagna noodles
- 1 tablespoon olive oil
- ½ onion, chopped
- 2 garlic cloves, minced
- 1 cup mozzarella cheese
- 1 cup ricotta cheese
- 15 oz. marinara sauce or Italian sauce
- 2 cups of water
- Salt, black pepper, to taste

How to make it:

1. Add oil to instant pot and press "sauté" button ("Normal" preset), wait till you see hot on the display. Add onion and garlic, cook for 2 minutes. Add beef, salt, and pepper, cook for 3-4 minutes.
2. Transfer instant pot content to a plate. Insert a trivet into the instant pot. Prepare a spring form pan that will fit into the instant pot.
3. Put lasagna pieces on the bottom of the pan. Add 1/3 part of sauce on top, 1/3 meat, mozzarella, and ricotta cheese.
4. Add another layer of pasta, sauce, and meat and cheese mixture. Repeat with the rest of the ingredients.
5. Add water to the instant pot. Put the spring form pan on a trivet.
6. Close the lid, and switch the vent to "sealed".
7. Press "pressure cook" (manual) button, use "+" or "-"button to set the timer for 20 minutes.
8. Use "pressure level" button to set the pressure to high.
9. Once the timer is up, press the "cancel" button and allow the pressure to be released naturally until the float valve drops down.
10. Open the lid. Serve warm.

Parmesan & Honey Pork Roast:

Serves: 2
Preparation Time: 5 minutes
Cooking Time: 35 minutes

Macros per serving:

Calories: 653
Protein: 71.4 grams
Fat: 29.4 grams
Carbohydrates: 20.5 grams

Ingredients:

- 1 pound pork roast
- 2 tablespoons parmesan cheese, grated
- 1 tablespoon soy sauce
- 2 tablespoons raw honey
- ½ tablespoon raw basil
- ½ tablespoon garlic, minced
- ½ tablespoon olive oil
- Salt to taste
- ½ tablespoon cornstarch
- ½ cup of water

How to make it:

1. Add all the ingredients to the instant pot, stir to mix well.
2. Secure the lid, pressure the MEAT/STEW button, and use the default time of 35 minutes.
3. When the cooking is complete, use a natural pressure release.
4. Serve hot.

Creamy Pork Treat:

Serves: 2
Preparation Time: 5-8 minutes
Cooking Time: 10 minutes

Macros per serving:

Calories: 376
Protein: 24.5 grams
Fat: 29.5 grams
Carbohydrates: 7 grams

Ingredients:

- 4 garlic cloves, minced
- 2 cups of milk
- 1 teaspoon thyme
- 1-pound pork sausage
- ¼ cup arrowroot
- ¼ teaspoon pepper
- ½ tablespoon olive oil
- ½ teaspoon salt

How to make it:

1. Take your instant pot; open the top lid. Plug it and turn it on.
2. Press "SAUTE" setting and the pot will start heating up.
3. In the cooking pot area, add the oil, garlic, and thyme. Cook until starts becoming translucent and softened for 1 minute. Stir in between.
4. Add sausage and cook it until it becomes brown. Make sure to break the sausage.
5. Pour 1 ½ cups the milk over it.
6. In a bowl, whisk together the arrowroot, remaining milk, salt, and pepper.
7. Close the top lid and seal its valve.
8. Press the "MANUAL" setting. Adjust cooking time to 5 minutes.
9. Allow the recipe to cook for the set cooking time.
10. After the set cooking time ends, press "CANCEL" and then press "QPR (Quick Pressure Release)".
11. Instant pot will quickly release the pressure.
12. Add the bowl mix and cook on "SAUTE" for 5 minutes.
13. Serve and enjoy!

Enchilada Pork tacos:

Serves: 2
Preparation Time: 5 minutes
Cooking Time: 45 minutes

Macros per serving:

Calories: 608
Protein: 44.7 grams
Fat: 29.6 grams
Carbohydrates: 19 grams

Ingredients:

- ½ cup chicken broth
- 1 pound pork shoulder roast, trimmed of fat
- ¼ cup enchilada sauce
- Taco shells, to serve
- Topping your choice like lettuce, tomatoes, cheese, etc.

How to make it:

1. Place your instant pot on a dry surface.
2. Open the lid; add the pork and broth and stir to combine using a wooden spatula.
3. Close the lid and ensure it's sealed properly.
4. Press MEAT/STEW; set timer to 35 minutes.
5. The instant pot will start building pressure; allow the mixture to cook for the set time.
6. After the timer reaches zero, turn venting knob from sealing to the venting position. Wait until float valve drops (1-2 minutes).
7. Remove the pork and discard the broth.
8. Cool down, shred and return to the instant pot.
9. Add enchilada sauce, press SAUTE, and simmer the mixture for 10 minutes.
10. Add the mixture to the taco shells.
11. Fill with toppings your choice and serve.

Pork Tenderloin Teriyaki:

Serves: 2
Preparation Time: 10 minutes
Cooking Time: 30 minutes

Macros per serving:

Calories: 270
Protein: 20 grams
Fat: 10 grams
Carbohydrates: 23 grams

Ingredients:

- 1 cup teriyaki sauce, mixed with water to thin out if too thick
- 1 green onion, chopped
- 1 pork tenderloins, sliced lengthwise into halves
- 1 tablespoon oil
- Salt and pepper
- Toasted sesame seeds

How to make it:

1. Generously season the pork with salt and pepper. Press the SAUTE key of the IP and put the oil in the inner pot. When the pot is hot, add the tenderloins. Cook until some of the sides are light brown. When the pork meat is browned, lay them down in the IP. Pour the teriyaki sauce over the top of the tenderloins.
2. Lock the lid and close the pressure valve. Set the IP to MANUAL high pressure for 20 minutes. NPR when the timer beeps. Open the lid and slice the meat. Serve with broccoli and cooked rice. Garnish with green onions and toasted sesame seeds.

Worcestershire Honey Pork:

Serves: 2
Preparation Time: 5 minutes
Cooking Time: 30 minutes
Macros per serving:

Calories: 442
Protein: 41.5 grams
Fat: 23.4 grams
Carbohydrates: 15.1 grams

Ingredients:

- ¾ pound pork loin
- 1 tablespoon olive oil
- 2 tablespoons honey
- 1 tablespoon Worcestershire sauce
- ½ lime, juiced
- 2 garlic cloves, minced
- 1 teaspoon fresh ginger, ground
- 1 tablespoon cornstarch or agar
- 1 cup of water
- Salt, pepper, to taste

How to make it:

1. Add oil to instant pot and press "SAUTE" button ("NORMAL" preset), wait till you see hot on the display, season pork with salt and pepper, then put into the instant pot. Cook for 2-5 minutes both sides. Press "cancel" button.
2. Mix honey, Worcestershire sauce, lime juice, garlic cloves and ginger in a bowl. Pour the mixture over pork, add water.
3. Close the lid, and switch the vent to "sealed".
4. Press the "meat/stew" button and accommodates "Less" planned. Once the timer is up press "cancel" button and turns the steam release handle to "venting" position for quick release until the float valve drops down.
5. Open the lid.
6. Transfer the pork to a plate and press "sauté" button, adjust to "less". Add cornstarch to the cooker.
7. Stir until the sauce thickens. Pour over the pork and serve.

Braised Lamb Shanks:

Serves: 4
Preparation Time: 10 minutes
Cooking Time: 35 minutes
Macros per serving:

Calories: 609
Protein: 66.5 grams
Fat: 24.0 grams
Carbohydrates: 18.4 grams

Ingredients:

- 2 pounds lamb shanks
- 4 tablespoons white flour
- 2 tablespoon olive oil
- 2 garlic cloves, diced
- 1 large onion, chopped
- 3 carrot, diced
- 2 tablespoon tomato paste
- 1 tomato, diced
- 1 teaspoon oregano
- 1 cup red wine
- ½ cup beef stock
- Salt and pepper to taste

How to make it:

1. In a shallow bowl, mix the flour and salt, and pepper.
2. Dredge the lamb shanks through the flour.
3. Set the moment pot to SAUTE and add the oil.
4. Sauté the lamb until browned and transfer to a plate.
5. In the remaining hot oil, sauté the garlic and onion for 5 minutes.
6. Mix in the tomato paste, diced tomato, red wine, and beef stock. Stir well and convey the mixture to a boil.
7. Return the lamb shanks to the instant pot. Close the lid and cook at low pressure for 25 minutes.
8. When the cooking is complete, use a natural pressure release.
9. Transfer the lamb shanks to a platter and top with cooking liquid.

Squash Wine Lamb Meal:

Serves: 2
Preparation Time: 10 minutes
Cooking Time: 50 minutes
Macros per serving:

Calories: 486
Protein: 39 grams
Fat: 29.5 grams
Carbohydrates: 43.5 grams

Ingredients:

- ½ butternut squash make medium size cubes
- 1 small onion, chopped
- 2 parsnips make medium size cubes
- 2 cloves garlic crushed
- ¼ cup white wine
- ¼ cup stock
- Olive's oil as needed
- Pepper and salt as needed
- ¾ pound lamb
- 2 carrots make medium size cubes

How to make it:

1. Take your 3-quart instant pot; open the top lid. Plug it and turn it on.
2. Press "SAUTE" setting and the pot will start heating up.
3. In the cooking pot area, add the meat. Stir and cook until evenly brown from all sides.
4. Add rest the ingredients and stir gently.
5. Close the top and seal its valve.
6. Press "MEAT/STEW" setting. Adjust cooking time to 45 minutes.
7. Allow the recipe to cook for the set cooking time.
8. After the set cooking time ends, press "CANCEL" and then press "QPR (Quick Pressure Release)".
9. Instant pot will quickly release the pressure.
10. Open the top lid, take out the meat and shred it.
11. Add back to the mix and combine; add the cooked recipe mix in serving plates.
12. Serve and enjoy!

Spinach Lentil Lamb:

Serves: 2
Preparation Time: 5 minutes
Cooking Time: 40-45 minutes
Macros per serving:

Calories: 522
Protein: 38.8 grams
Fat: 21.1 grams
Carbohydrates: 37.3 grams

Ingredients:

- 1/3 pound spinach, chopped
- 1 medium onion, sliced
- 1 ½ teaspoons ginger, minced
- ½ pound lamb, cubed
- ¼ pound red lentils, dried and rinsed
- ½ cup chicken stock
- 1 ½ teaspoon curry powder
- ½ teaspoon chili powder
- ½ teaspoon ground cumin
- ½ teaspoon ground coriander
- ¼ teaspoon turmeric powder
- 1½ cloves garlic, minced
- ½ can tomatoes, crushed
- Cooking oil as needed
- Salt to taste

How to make it:

1. Mix all the spices in a mixing bowl and use half of the spice mix to rub the lamb evenly.
2. Place your instant pot on a dry surface and open the lid.
3. Press SAUTE; add the oil and heat it.
4. Add the seasoned lamb; cook to soften and evenly brown.
5. Remove lamb and set aside.
6. Add the onion, garlic, and ginger;
7. Cook until the onions are translucent.
8. Add the remaining ingredients and lamb. Add enough water to cover the ingredients.
9. Close the lid and check that it's sealed properly.
10. Press MANUAL; set timer to 35 minutes.
11. The instant pot will start building pressure; allow the mixture to cook for the set time.
12. After the timer reaches zero, wait for the float valve to drop. It will take 8-10 minutes.
13. Open the lid and transfer the food to a plate.
14. Divide among serving plates/bowls; serve warm.

Braised Lamb with Tomatoes and Carrots:

Serves: 2
Preparation Time: 20 minutes
Cooking Time: 30 minutes
Macros per serving:

Calories: 703
Protein: 72 grams
Fat: 38 grams
Carbohydrates: 18 grams

Ingredients:

- 1 ½ sprigs fresh oregano, chopped
- 1 ½ sprigs fresh rosemary, chopped
- 1 ½ sprigs fresh thyme, chopped
- 1 carrot, peeled and sliced
- 1 cup canned whole tomatoes, sliced
- 1 pound lamb shanks
- ½ white onion, large
- 3 cloves garlic, sliced
- 3 tablespoons oil
- 4 cups veal or beef stock
- Flour, for dredging
- Salt and pepper.

How to make it:

1. Set the IP to SAUTE. Dredge the lamb with flour. Put the oil in the inner pot. Add the lamb. Cook until browned. Except for the whole tomatoes, add the rest of the ingredients.
2. Press the CANCEL key. Lock the lid and close the pressure valve. Set the IP to Manual high pressure for 25 minutes. QPR when the timer beeps.
3. Open the lid. Add the tomatoes.
4. Lock the lid and close the pressure valve. Set the IP top MANUAL high pressure for 5 minutes. QPR when the timer beeps. Open the lid, serve.

Spiced Potato Lamb Dinner:

Serves: 2
Preparation Time: 10 minutes
Cooking Time: 35 minutes
Macros per serving:

Calories: 371
Protein: 33.5 grams
Fat: 13.4 grams
Carbohydrates: 31 grams

Ingredients:

- 1 tomato, chopped
- ½ pound rack of lamb
- ½ pound baby potatoes
- 1 carrot, chopped
- 1 cup chicken stock
- ½ onion, chopped
- 1 cheery stalk, chopped
- A pinch of rosemary, dried
- 1 tablespoon ketchup
- 1 tablespoon beef broth
- 2 garlic cloves, minced
- A pinch of pepper and salt
- 1 teaspoon sweet paprika
- 1 teaspoon cumin, ground
- A pinch of oregano, dried

How to make it:

1. Take your 3-quart instant pot; open the top lid. Plug it and turn it on.
2. In the cooking pot area, add the baby potatoes, carrot, onion, celery, tomato, stock, garlic, salt, pepper, paprika, cumin, oregano, rosemary, ketchup, lamb, and beef broth. Using a spatula, stir the ingredients.
3. Close the top lid and seal its valve.
4. Press the "MANUAL" setting. Adjust cooking time to 35 minutes.
5. Allow the recipe to cook set cooking time.
6. After the set cooking time ends, press "CANCEL" and then press "QPR (quick pressure release)".
7. Instant pot will quickly release the pressure.
8. Open the top lid and the cooked recipe mix in serving plates.
9. Serve and enjoy!

Seafood & Fish Recipes

Ginger-Lemon Haddock:

Serves: 2
Preparation time: 5 minutes
Cooking time: 8 minutes
Macros per serving:

Calories: 274
Protein: 32.2 grams
Fat: 8.7 grams
Carbohydrates: 5.7 grams

Ingredients:

- 4 fillets of haddock
- 2 lemons
- 1-inch fresh ginger, chopped
- 4 green onions
- 1 cup white wine
- Salt and pepper to taste
- 2 tablespoons olive oil

How to make it:

1. Massage the olive oil into the fish filets and sprinkle them with salt and pepper.
2. Juice your lemons and zest one of them.
3. Add that to the instant pot with the wine, onions, and ginger
4. Place the fish in a steamer basket and lower it to the liquid.
5. Close the lid and cook at air mass for eight minutes.
6. When cookery is complete, does a fast pressure unharness.
7. Remove the fish and serve on rice or with a big salad.

Olive Cod Mystery:

Serves: 2
Preparation time: 5-8 minutes
Cooking time: 10 minutes
Macros per serving:

Calories: 185
Protein: 7 grams
Fat: 3 grams
Carbohydrates: 6 grams

Ingredients:

- 1 cup of water
- 2 tablespoons capers, chopped
- 1 cup black olives, pitted and chopped
- 17 ounces cherry tomatoes, halved
- 4 cod fillets, boneless and skinless
- 1 garlic clove, minced
- 1 tablespoon olive oil
- A pinch of pepper and salt
- 1 tablespoon parsley, finely chopped

How to make it:

1. In a heatproof dish, mix the tomato salt, pepper, parsley, oil, fish, olive capers, and garlic. Toss to combine well.
2. Switch on your instant pot after placing it on a clean and dry kitchen platform.
3. Pour the water into the cooking pot area. Arrange the trivet inside it; arrange the dish over the trivet.
4. Close the pot by closing the top lid. Also, ensure to seal the valve.
5. Press "manual" cooking function and set the cooking time to 8 minutes. It will start cooking after a few minutes. Let the pot mix cook under pressure until the timer reads zero.
6. Turn off and press "cancel" cooking function. Quick-release pressure.
7. Open the pot and serve on a serving plate or bowl. Enjoy the Paleo dish!

Tomato Herbed Fish:

Serves: 2
Preparation time: 5 minutes
Cooking time: 3 minutes
Macros per serving:

Calories: 412
Protein: 14.2 grams
Fat: 39 grams
Carbohydrates: 12.6 grams

Ingredients:

- 4 cherry tomatoes, halved
- 1 tablespoon pickled capers
- 1 clove garlic, smashed
- 1/3 cup olives, pitted, sliced
- 2 white fish fillets
- 1 teaspoon olive oil
- ½ teaspoon dried thyme
- Black pepper and salt, to taste

How to make it:

1. To a brisket or steamer basket, add all the ingredients.
2. Place your instant pot on a dry surface and open the lid.
3. Add 1 cup water and arrange the brisket or steamer basket over it.
4. Close the lid and make certain it's sealed properly.
5. Press MANUAL; set timer to 3 minutes.
6. The instant pot will start building pressure; allow the mixture to cook for the set time.
7. After the timer reaches zero, turn venting knob from sealing to the venting position. Wait until float valve drops (1-2 minutes).
8. Open the lid and transfer the food to a plate.
9. Divide among serving plates/bowls; serve warm.

Wild Alaskan Cod:

Serves: 2
Preparation time: 5 minutes
Cooking time: 5-9 minutes
Macros per serving:

Calories: 60
Protein: 0 grams
Fat: 6 grams
Carbohydrates: 2 grams

Ingredients:

- 1 cup cherry tomatoes
- 1 large filet wild Alaskan cod, sliced into 2 pieces
- 2 tablespoons butter
- Salt and pepper
- Seasoning of choice
- Drizzle olive oil

How to make it:

1. Get an oven-safe glass dish that will fit the IP. Put the tomatoes on the bottom of the dish. Put the fish on top of the tomatoes. Season with pepper, salt, and choice of seasoning. Tap each with 1 tablespoon butter and drizzle with oil.
2. Put the IP trivet pour 1 cup of water in the inner pot. Set the dish on the trivet. Lock the lid and close the pressure valve. Set the IP to MANUAL high pressure for 5 minutes for thawed or for 9 minutes for frozen fish. QPR when the timer beeps.

Buttery Shrimp Paella:

Serves: 2
Preparation time: 5 minutes
Cooking time: 7 minutes

Macros per serving:

Calories: 603
Protein: 31.3 grams
Fat: 13 grams
Carbohydrates: 41.2 grams

Ingredients:

- 1 cup risotto rice
- ½ lb. big shrimps. Deveined
- 2 tablespoons butter
- 1 small onion, chopped
- 1 cup chicken broth
- ¼ cup white wine
- ¼ cup parsley, chopped
- A pinch of saffron
- 1 lemon, quartered
- 2 garlic cloves, minced
- A pinch of red pepper, crushed
- A pinch of sea salt
- Black pepper, to taste

How to make it:

1. Add butter to instant pot and press "sauté" button ("Normal" preset), wait till you see hot on the display.
2. Add onion to the pot and cook until soft. Add garlic and cook for one more minutes. Add red pepper, saffron, salt, and black pepper.
3. Add rice and stir for about 1 minute. Add broth and wine; press the "cancel" button. Put the shrimp on top.
4. Close the lid, and turn the vent to "sealed".
5. Press "pressure cook" (Manual) button, use "+" or "-"button to set the timer for 5 minutes. Use "pressure level" button to set the pressure to high.
6. Once the timer is up press "Cancel" button and turns the steam release handle to "venting" position for quick release until the float valve drops down.
7. Open the lid. Serve with parsley and lemon wedges on top.

Glazed Salmon:

Serves: 2
Preparation time: 15 minutes
Cooking time: 5 minutes
Macros per serving:

Calories: 290
Protein: 28.1 grams
Fat: 16 grams
Carbohydrates: 10.9 grams

Ingredients:

- 2 (5-ounce) salmon fillets
- Salt and pepper to taste
- 1 jalapeno pepper, seeded and finely chopped
- 2 garlic cloves, minced
- 1 tablespoon fresh parsley, chopped
- 2 tablespoons fresh lime juice
- 1 tablespoon olive oil
- 1 tablespoon honey
- 1 tablespoon hot water
- ½ teaspoon ground cumin
- ½ teaspoon paprika

How to make it:

1. Season the salmon fillets with salt and black pepper evenly.
2. For the sauce: in a bowl, add remaining ingredients and mix until well combined.
3. Arrange a steamer trivet in the instant pot. Add 1 cup of water in instant pot.
4. Place the salmon fillets on top of the trivet.
5. Secure the lid. Press the STEAM button, and cook for 5 minutes.
6. After cooking is complete, do a quick pressure release.
7. Remove the lid and transfer the salmon filets onto serving plates.
8. Drizzle with sauce and serve.

Mussels Tomatino:

Serves: 2
Preparation time: 8-10 minutes
Cooking time: 3 minutes
Macros per serving:

Calories: 446
Protein: 55 grams
Fat: 10.5 grams
Carbohydrates: 22.5 grams

Ingredients:

- ½ cup white wine
- ½ tablespoon dried parsley
- ½ tablespoon pepper
- 2 pounds fresh mussels, cleaned and rinsed
- 1 cup diced tomatoes
- Salt as per taste preference

How to make it:

1. Switch on the pot after placing it on a clean and dry platform.
2. Pour the tomatoes into the instant pot with the juices and add the wine. Add the pepper, salt, and parsley.
3. Place the mussels in a steamer basket and lower it to the liquid.
4. Close the pot by closing the top lid. Also, ensure to seal the valve.
5. Press "Manual" cooking function and set the cooking time to 3 minutes. It will start cooking after a few minutes. Let the pot mix cook under pressure until the timer reads zero.
6. Press "cancel" preparation operates and press "quick release" setting.
7. Open the pot and serve warm with garlic bread. Enjoy it with your loved one!

Wine Braised Calamari:

Serves: 2
Preparation Time: 5 minutes
Cooking Time: 4 minutes

Macros per serving:

Calories: 483
Protein: 42.7 grams
Fat: 9.2 grams
Carbohydrates: 12.7 grams

Ingredients:

- 1 sprig rosemary
- 2 tablespoons Italian parsley Chopped
- 1 celery stalk, chopped
- 1 pound calamari, chopped
- ½ cup red wine
- 1 garlic clove, chopped
- 1 cup tomatoes, crushed
- 1 tablespoon olive oil
- ½ red onion, sliced
- Chopped parsley, to serve
- Black pepper and salt, to taste

How to make it:

1. In a bowl, toss the calamari pieces with olive oil, pepper, and salt.
2. Place your instant pot on a dry surface.
3. Open the lid; add the wine, tomatoes, celery, rosemary, garlic, and red onion. Stir the mixture.
4. Add the calamari to a steamer basket and lower it to the liquid.
5. Close the lid and certify it's sealed properly.
6. Press MANUAL; set timer to 4 minutes.
7. The instant pot will start building pressure; allow the mixture to cook for the set time.
8. After the timer reaches zero, turn venting knob from sealing to the venting position. Wait until float valve drops (1-2 minutes).
9. Open the lid and transfer the food to a plate.
10. Divide among serving plates/bowls; top with some parsley and serve warm.

Black Bean and Rice Shrimp:

Serves: 2
Preparation Time: 10 minutes
Cooking Time: 15 minutes
Macros per serving:

Calories: 390
Protein: 31 grams
Fat: 14 grams
Carbohydrates: 36 grams

Ingredients:

- 1 ½ cups broth or water
- 1 can black beans, rinsed and drained
- 1 cup of rice
- ½ pound cooked or raw frozen shrimp
- ¼ cup butter
- 2 tablespoons minced garlic
- Fresh or freeze-dried cilantro
- Salt and pepper to taste
- Splash of lime juice
- Splash of coconut oil

How to make it:

1. Press the SAUTE key. Add the butter and melt. Add the rice and sauté until browned.
2. Add the pepper, salt, and garlic, and cook until fragrant. Add the rest of the ingredients.
3. Lock the lid and close the pressure valve. Set the IP to MANUAL high pressure for 5 minutes. QPR when the timer beeps.
4. Serve topped with cilantro.

Orange Scallop Mania:

Serves: 2
Preparation Time: 5 minutes
Cooking Time: 6 minutes
Macros per serving:

Calories: 293
Protein: 20 grams
Fat: 27.1 grams
Carbohydrates: 13.8 grams

Ingredients:

- ½ lb. sea scallops, cleaned
- ½ jalapeno pepper, seedless and minced
- 3 tablespoons extra virgin olive oil
- 1 tablespoon rice vinegar
- ¼ teaspoon mustard
- 1/3 cup water or broth
- 2 oranges, sliced
- Salt, black pepper, to taste
- A pinch cayenne pepper

How to make it:

1. Pulse jalapeno with 2 tablespoons olive oil, mustard, black pepper, salt and vinegar in a blender. Season scallops with cayenne pepper.
2. Add 1 tablespoon oil to instant pot and pressure "sauté" button ("Normal" preset), wait till you see hot on the display. Add scallops and cook them with the lid open for 3 minutes on each side.
3. Press "cancel" button. Add water or broth, jalapeno sauce, orange slices and close the lid, turn the vent to "sealed"
4. Press "pressure cook" (manual) button, use "+" or "-"button to set the timer for 6 minutes. Use "pressure level" button to set the pressure to high.
5. Once the timer is up to the pressure "cancel" button and turns the steam release handle to "venting" position for quick release until the float valve drops down.
6. Open the lid and enjoy.

Fish Curry:

Serves: 2
Preparation Time: 15 minutes
Cooking Time: 11 minutes
Macros per serving:

Calories: 787
Protein: 29.7 grams
Fat: 57.6 grams
Carbohydrates: 47.2 grams

Ingredients:

- 1 tablespoon olive oil
- 1 medium onion, chopped
- 1 teaspoon fresh ginger, grated finely
- 2 garlic cloves, Minced
- 1 tablespoon curry powder
- 1 teaspoon ground cumin
- 1 teaspoon ground coriander
- ½ teaspoon red chili powder
- ¼ teaspoon ground turmeric
- 1 cup unsweetened coconut milk
- ¾ pound fish fillets, cut into bite-sized pieces
- ½ cup tomatoes, chopped
- 1 Serrano pepper, seeded and chopped
- ½ tablespoon fresh lemon juice

How to make it:

1. Place the oil within the instant pot and choose SAUTE. Add the onion, ginger, and garlic and cook for 4-5 minutes.
2. Add the spices and cook for 1 minute.
3. The coconut milk and stir to mix well.
4. Press CANCEL and stir in the fish, tomatoes, and Serrano pepper.
5. Secure the lid and cook at low pressure for 5 minutes.
6. When preparation is complete, use a natural pressure unharness.
7. Remove the lid and stir in the lemon juice.
8. Serve hot.

White Wine Haddock:

Serves: 2
Preparation Time: 5-8 minutes
Cooking Time: 8 minutes

Macros per serving:

Calories: 274
Protein: 32 grams
Fat: 8.5 grams
Carbohydrates: 5.5 grams

Ingredients:

- 4 green onions
- 1 cup white wine
- 4 fillets of haddock
- 2 lemons
- Pepper and salt as per taste preference
- 2 tablespoons olive oil
- 1-inch fresh ginger, chopped

How to make it:

1. Rub the olive oil the fish fillets and sprinkle them with pepper and salt.
2. Juice your lemons and zest one lemon.
3. Switch on the pot after placing it on a clean and dry platform.
4. Open the pot lid and place everything except fish in the cooking pot area. Give the ingredients a little stir.
5. Place the fish in a steamer basket and lower it to the liquid. Close the pot by closing the top lid. Also, ensure to seal the valve.
6. Press "Manual" cooking function and set the cooking time to 8 minutes. It will start cooking after a few minutes. Let the pot mix cook under pressure until the timer reads zero.
7. Pressure "cancel" change of state performs and press "quick release" setting.
8. Open the pot and serve warm with the veggie salad or rice. Enjoy it with your loved one!

Honey Lemon Salmon:

Serves: 2
Preparation Time: 5 minutes
Cooking Time: 5 minutes
Macros per serving:

Calories: 361
Protein: 27.1 grams
Fat: 21.3 grams
Carbohydrates: 16.4 grams

Ingredients:

- 1 tablespoon honey
- 1 tablespoon hot water
- 1 tablespoon olive oil
- 2 5-ounce salmon fillets
- 1 cup of water
- Juice of 1 lime
- ½ teaspoon paprika
- 1 jalapeno, seeded and minced
- ½ teaspoon cumin
- Black pepper and salt, to taste

How to make it:

1. In a medium bowl, thoroughly whisk the lime juice with honey, hot water, olive oil, cumin, a pinch black pepper (ground) and salt.
2. Place your instant pot on a dry surface and open the lid.
3. Add the water to the pot and arrange a trivet or steamer basket over it.
4. Season the salmon with a pinch black pepper (ground) and salt.
5. Place the salmon fillets on the trivet.
6. Close the lid and certify it's sealed properly.
7. Press MANUAL; set timer to 5 minutes.
8. The instant pot will start building pressure; allow the mixture to cook for the set time.
9. After the timer reaches zero, turn venting knob from sealing to the venting position. Wait until float valve drops (1-2 minutes).
10. Open the lid.
11. Serve the cooked salmon fillets with the bowl sauce.

Perfectly Steamed Crab Legs

Serves: 2
Preparation Time: 5 minutes
Cooking Time: 3 minutes

Macros per serving:

Calories: 340
Protein: 41 grams
Fat: 18 grams
Carbohydrates: 3 grams

Ingredients:

- 1 cup of water
- 1 pound wild-caught snow legs, slightly Thawed
- 1/3 cup melted salted butter or ghee
- Lemon slices

How to make it:

1. Put the IP trivet or steamer basket and pour 1 cup of water in the inner pot.
2. Put the crab legs on the trivet. Lock the lid and close the pressure valve.
3. Set the IP to MANUAL high pressure for 3 minutes.
4. QPR when the timer beeps.
5. Using tongs, carefully transfer the crab legs onto a serving platter. Serve with the lemon slices and melted butter or ghee.

Notes: Don't throw the leftover shells. Make a carb stock. Just put all the shells back in the IP- no need to wash. Add enough water to cover the shells. Lock the lid and close the pressure valve. Set the IP to Manual high pressure for 60 minutes. QPR or NPR when the timer beeps Refrigerate and use within 3 days or freeze if not using within that period.

Spicy Saucy Crab Cakes:

Serves: 2
Preparation Time: 5 minutes
Cooking Time: 8 minutes

Macros per serving:

Calories: 472
Protein: 21.1 grams
Fat: 27.4 grams
Carbohydrates: 31.9 grams

Ingredients:

- ½ cup jarred roasted red pepper and garlic sauce
- ¼ cup mayonnaise
- 1 tablespoon lemon juice
- 2 tablespoons butter
- ¼ cup of water

For crab cakes:

- ½ pound crab meat, free of shells
- ¼ cup breadcrumbs
- ½ teaspoon salt
- ¼ teaspoon white pepper
- ¼ teaspoon paprika
- 1 egg
- 2 tablespoons fresh parsley, chopped
- 3 tablespoons flour

How to make it:

1. Mix all crab cakes ingredients in a bowl and shape the mixture into flat cakes. Add butter to instant pot and press "sauté" button ("normal" preset). Wait till you see hot on the display.
2. Cook crab cakes for about 3 minutes on each side or until lightly browned. Mix red pepper and garlic sauce, mayonnaise and water in a bowl, pour into the pressure cooker. Press "cancel" button.
3. Close the lid, and switch the vent to "sealed".
4. Press "pressure cook" (manual) button, use "+" or "-"button to set the timer for 5 minutes. Use "pressure level" button to set the pressure to high.
5. Once the timer is up press "cancel" button and turns the steam release handle to "venting" position for quick release until the float valve drops down.
6. Open the lid and serve.

Vegetables Recipes

Butternut Squash Risotto:

Serves: 2
Preparation Time: 10 minutes
Cooking Time: 7 minutes
Macros per serving:

Calories: 412
Protein: 13.2 grams
Fat: 5.6 grams
Carbohydrates: 75.5 grams

Ingredients:

- 1 tablespoon vegetable oil
- 1 white onion, finely chopped
- 1 red bell pepper, chopped
- 1 cup chopped button mushrooms
- 3 garlic cloves, minced
- 3 ½ cups of vegetable broth
- 1½ cups risotto rice, rinsed
- ¼ cup white wine
- Some ground pepper
- 2 cups butternut squash, peeled and diced
- 3 cups of assorted greens (spinach, kale, and chard)
- 1 tablespoon nutritional yeast

How to make it:

1. Place the oil within the instant pot and choose SAUTE.
2. Add garlic, onions, and bell pepper, and sauté until they turn slightly soft.
3. Throw in the rice and stir well.
4. Pour the vegetable broth into the pot, followed by the wine, chopped mushrooms, salt, and pepper, and mix well.
5. Close the lid and cook at high pressure for 7 minutes.
6. When the cooking is complete, do a natural pressure release.
7. Transfer the risotto into bowls. Sprinkle nutritional yeast on top and stir. The mixture will thicken shortly, and ready to serve.

Wholesome Asparagus Appetizer:

Serves: 2
Preparation Time: 2-3 minutes
Cooking Time: 2 minutes

Macros per serving:

Calories: 69
Protein: 3 grams
Fat: 6.5 grams
Carbohydrates: 4 grams

Ingredients:

- 2 tablespoons olive oil
- 1 tablespoon onion
- Sea pepper and salt as needed
- 1 cup of water
- 1 pound asparagus

How to make it:

1. Arrange your instant pot over a dry, clean platform. Plug it in the power socket and turn it on.
2. Slowly pour the water into the pot order to avoid spilling out. Take the trivet and arrange in the pot; place the asparagus over the trivet.
3. Drizzle them with the olive oil and onion.
4. Close the lid and lock. Ensure that you have sealed the valve to avoid leakage.
5. Press "Manual" mode from available cooking settings and set the cooking time to 2 minutes. Instant pot will start cooking the ingredients after a few minutes.
6. After the timer reads zero, press "Cancel" and quick-release pressure.
7. Carefully remove the lid, season as needed and serve the prepared keto dish warm!

Chickpea Tofu Pasta:

Serves: 2
Preparation Time: 10 minutes
Cooking Time: 25 minutes
Macros per serving:

Calories: 512
Protein: 21.8 grams
Fat: 9 grams
Carbohydrates: 45.3 grams

Ingredients:

- 1 medium tomato, chopped
- 1 apple, chopped
- 1 cup chickpeas
- 1 cup cooked elbow pasta
- ½ cup tofu, chopped
- 1 small green bell pepper, chopped
- Salt to taste

For the dressing:

- 1 clove garlic, minced
- ½ teaspoon red chili flakes
- 4 teaspoons apple cider vinegar
- 1 tablespoon honey
- 1 teaspoon dried oregano
- Black pepper and salt, to taste

How to make it:

1. Soak the chickpeas in water overnight; drain and put aside.
2. In a medium bowl, thoroughly combine the dressing ingredients.
3. Place your instant pot on a dry surface.
4. Open the lid; add the chickpeas, salt and enough water to cover the chickpeas.
5. Close the lid and ensure its sealed properly.
6. Press MANUAL; set timer to 25 minutes.
7. The instant pot will start building pressure; allow the mixture to cook for the set time.
8. After the timer reaches zero, turn venting knob from sealing to the venting position. Wait until float valve drops (1-2 minutes).
9. Open the lid and transfer the cooked mixture to a plate.
10. Add the tomatoes, tofu, apple, and bell pepper. Season as needed and toss well.
11. Top with the dressing.
12. Divide among serving plates/bowls; serve warm.

Cauliflower and Sweet Potato Mash:

Serves: 2
Preparation Time: 15 minutes
Cooking Time: 25 minutes
Macros per serving:

Calories: 313
Protein: 8 grams
Fat: 1 gram
Carbohydrates: 71 grams

Ingredients:

- 1½ tablespoons milk of choice
- 1 pound sweet potatoes, peeled, chopped into 1 ½-inch cube
- ½ pound cauliflower florets
- ¼ teaspoon garlic powder
- 1/8 cup plain Greek yogurt
- Chopped fresh parsley, for garnish
- Salt and pepper to taste

How to make it:

1. Pour 1-inch level worth of water in the inner pot and put the IP steamer basket. Put the sweet potatoes and cauliflower on the steamer.
2. Lock the lid and close the pressure valve. Set the IP to MANUAL high pressure for 10 to 12 minutes or until fork-tender. QPR when the timer beeps. Open the lid.
3. Transfer the cooked cauliflower and potato in a large mixing bowl. Add the milk mash until combined completely.
4. Add the yogurt, pepper, salt, and garlic powder. Stir to combine.
5. If the mash is too thick, add 1 tablespoon milk at a time until desired consistency is achieved. Serve garnished with parsley.

Eggplant Olive Crush:

Serves: 2
Preparation Time: 5 minutes
Cooking Time: 20 minutes
Macros per serving:

Calories: 175
Protein: 12.7 grams
Fat: 14 grams
Carbohydrates: 13.1 grams

Ingredients:

- 2 eggplants, peeled from one side only, chopped
- 1 cup of water
- 2 tablespoons olive oil
- ¼ cup black olives pitted
- 1 tablespoon tahini
- 2 garlic cloves
- 2 tablespoons squeezed lemon juice
- 1 teaspoon salt
- 1 tablespoon fresh thyme levels

How to make it:

1. Add oil to instant pot and press "sauté" button ("normal" preset), wait till you see hot on the display.
2. Add eggplant, fry and caramelize from all sides, for about 5 minutes with the lid open. Press "cancel" button.
3. Add garlic, water, and salt.
4. Closed the lid and turn the vent to "sealed".
5. Press (manual) button, use + or - button to set the timer for 3 minutes. Use "pressure level" button to set the pressure to high.
6. Once the timer is up, press the "cancel" button and allow the pressure to be released and allow the pressure to be released naturally, until the float valve drops down. Open the lid.
7. Discard most of the liquid from the pot. Get garlic cloves and remove the skin. Put them back to the pot; add lemon juice, black olives, and tahini.
8. Use an immersion blender to make a puree. Transfer to a bowl.
9. Sprinkle with a dash of olive oil and thyme before serving.

Rice & Lentils with Veggies:

Serves: 2
Preparation Time: 20 minutes
Cooking Time: 10 minutes
Macros per serving:

Calories: 356
Protein: 20.3 grams
Fat: 17.9 grams
Carbohydrates: 93 grams

Ingredients:

- 1 tablespoon olive oil
- ½ teaspoon cumin seeds
- ½ of a small onion, chopped
- ½ tablespoon fresh ginger paste
- 1 small potato, cut into small pieces
- ½ cup carrots, peeled and diced
- ½ cup fresh green peas shelled
- 1 tomato, chopped finely
- ¼ teaspoon red chili powder
- ¼ teaspoon ground turmeric
- Salt to taste
- ½ cup white rice, rinsed
- ½ cup split green lentils, rinsed
- 3 cups of water
- 1 tablespoon fresh cilantro, chopped

How to make it:

1. Place the oil within the instant pot and choose SAUTE. Add the cumin seeds and cook for thirty seconds.
2. Add the onions and ginger and cook for about 2 minutes.
3. Add vegetables and spices and cook for 2 minutes.
4. Press CANCEL and stir in remaining ingredients, except cilantro.
5. Secure the lid and cook at air mass for five minutes.
6. When the cooking is complete, do a natural pressure release for 10 minutes. Quick-release the remaining pressure.
7. Serve with the garnishing of cilantro.

Cheesy Asparagus:

Serves: 2
Preparation Time: 5-8 minutes
Cooking Time: 2 minutes
Macros per serving:

Calories: 113
Protein: 4.5 grams
Fat: 12.5 grams
Carbohydrates: 6 grams

Ingredients:

- 1 tablespoon olive oil
- ½ cup of water
- ½ teaspoon of sea salt
- 9-ounce asparagus make halves
- 1 tablespoon sesame seeds
- ½ garlic clove, chopped
- Cheddar, shredded as needed

How to make it:

1. Take your instant pot; open the top lid. Plug it and turn it on.
2. In the cooking pot area, add the water, garlic, salt, oil sesame seeds, and asparagus. Using a spatula, stir the ingredients.
3. Close the top lid and seal its valve.
4. Press "STEAM" setting. Adjust cooking time to 2 minutes.
5. Allow the recipe to cook for the set cooking time.
6. After the set cooking time ends, press "CANCEL" and then press "QPR (Quick Pressure Release)".
7. Instant pot will quickly release the pressure.
8. Open the top lid; add the cooked recipe mix in serving plates.
9. Top with some shredded cheese.

Parmesan Spinach Pasta:

Serves: 2
Preparation Time: 5 minutes
Cooking Time: 11 minutes

Macros per serving:

Calories: 486
Protein: 21 grams
Fat: 18 grams
Carbohydrates: 51.2 grams

Ingredients:

- 2 cups chopped
- 2 clove garlic, minced
- ½ pounds fusilli pasta, whole wheat
- 2 tablespoons butter, cubed
- 2 ½ cups water
- Black pepper and salt, to taste
- 1/3 cup parmesan, grated

How to make it:

1. Place your instant pot on a dry surface.
2. Open the lid; add the water and pasta. Add the spinach and garlic over it.
3. Stir to combine using a wooden spatula.
4. Close the lid and make certain it's sealed properly.
5. Press MANUAL; set timer to 6 minutes.
6. The instant pot will start building pressure; allow the mixture to cook for the set time.
7. After the timer reaches zero, turn venting knob from sealing to the venting position. Wait until float valve drops (1-2 minutes).
8. Open the lid and add the seasoning, butter, and cheese; combine and set aside for 5 minutes.
9. Divide among serving plates/bowls, serve warm.

Root Vegetable Mash:

Serves: 2
Preparation Time: 20 minutes
Cooking Time: 30 minutes
Macros per serving:

Calories: 300
Protein: 2 grams
Fat: 27 grams
Carbohydrates: 15 grams

Ingredients:

- 4 root vegetables, (turnips, sweet potato, radishes, carrot, rutabaga, etc.), thick-skinned pieces peeled, cubed
- ¼ cup of coconut oil
- ½ tablespoon coarse sea salt
- ½ large onion, coarsely chopped
- ½ head garlic, sliced in half to expose the center of the cloves

How to make it:

1. Put the root veggies; garlic, onion, ½ of the coconut oil, and 1 cup water in the inner pot.
2. Lock the lid and close the pressure valve. Set the IP to manual high pressure for 10 minutes.
3. NPR when the timer beeps. Open the lid. Sprinkle with salt.
4. Add the remaining coconut oil. Stir to coat. With a slotted spoon, transfer the mixture into a food processor. Puree until smooth, serve.

Apple Cabbage Delight:

Serves: 2
Preparation Time: 5 minutes
Cooking Time: 7 minutes
Macros per serving:

Calories: 85
Protein: 1.4 grams
Fat: 1.7 grams
Carbohydrates: 17.9 grams

Ingredients:

- 3 cups red cabbage, chopped
- ½ cup unsweetened apple sauce
- 1 cup of water
- 1 onion, chopped
- 1 teaspoon olive oil
- 1 teaspoon apple cider vinegar
- 1 teaspoon honey
- Salt and pepper, to taste

How to make it:

1. And oil to instant pot and press "sauté" button wait till you see hot on the show.
2. Add onion and cook for 3-4 minute until soft. Press "cancel" button. Add cabbage, apple sauce, vinegar, cider, water, salt, and pepper.
3. Close the lid, and switch the vent to "sealed".
4. Press "pressure cook" (manual) button, use "+" or "-"button to set the timer for 3 minutes. Use "pressure level" button to set the pressure to high.
5. Once the timer is up press "cancel" button and turns the steam release handle to "venting" position for quick release until the float valve drops down.
6. Open the lid. Serve warm.

Curried Edamame:

Serves: 2
Preparation Time: 15 minutes
Cooking Time: 18 minutes
Macros per serving:

Calories: 586
Protein: 29.4 grams
Fat: 40 grams
Carbohydrates: 37.9 grams

Ingredients:

- 2 teaspoons coconut oil
- 1 teaspoon black mustard seeds
- ¼ teaspoon fennel seeds
- ¼ teaspoon fenugreek seeds
- 10 curry leaves, chopped roughly
- ½ cup red onion, chopped
- 4 garlic clove, chopped
- 2 medium tomatoes, chopped
- 1 teaspoon tamarind paste
- 2 teaspoons ground coriander
- ¾ teaspoon cayenne pepper
- 1 ½ cups fresh edamame
- ¾ cup of coconut milk
- 1 cup of water
- Salt and pepper to taste

How to make it:

1. Place the coconut oil in the instant pot and select SAUTE. Add all the seeds and cook for 1 minute.
2. Add the curry leaves, onion, and garlic and cook for about 4 minutes.
3. Add the tomato, tamarind, and spices and cook for 4-5 minutes.
4. Press the CANCEL button and stir in remaining ingredients.
5. Secure the lid and cook at air mass for seven minutes.
6. When the cooking is complete, carefully do a quick pressure release.
7. Serve hot.

Bacon Honey Sprouts:

Serves: 2
Preparation Time: 5 minutes
Cooking Time: 8-10 minutes

Macros per serving:

Calories: 57
Protein: 4 grams
Fat: 8.5 grams
Carbohydrates: 6 grams

Ingredients:

- 1 tablespoon honey
- 4 slices of bacon, chopped
- ½ cup of water
- Sea salt as needed
- 4 cup Brussels sprouts, chopped

How to make it:

1. Arrange your instant pot over a dry, clean platform. Plug it in the power socket and turn it on.
2. Now press "sauté" mode from available option. In the cooking area, add the bacon; cook for 4-5 minutes to crisp it.
3. Add the sprouts and cook for 4-5 more minutes. Pour the water.
4. Close the lid and lock. Ensure that you have sealed the valve to avoid leakage.
5. Press "manual" mode from available cooking setting and set the cooking time to 2 minutes. Instant pot will start cooking the ingredients after a few minutes.
6. After the timer reads zero, press "cancel" and quick-release pressure.
7. Carefully remove the lid and serve the prepared keto dish warm! Add some salt if needed.

Mixed Veggie Rice Meal:

Serves: 2
Preparation Time: 5 minutes
Cooking Time: 14-18 minutes

Macros per serving:

Calories: 456
Protein: 11 grams
Fat: 13.4 grams
Carbohydrates: 46.7 grams

Ingredients:

- 1 cup basmati rice
- 1 medium onion, sliced
- ¼ cup mint levels, chopped
- 1 tablespoon oil
- ½ teaspoon ginger, crushed
- ½ teaspoon garlic, crushed
- ½ cup yogurt + extra to serve
- 1 tablespoon garam masala
- 1 ½ cups mixed vegetables your choice, chopped
- 1 teaspoon salt
- 1½ cups water
- 2 tablespoons toasted cashews, chopped

How to make it:

1. Soak the rice in water for 20 minutes; drain and set aside.
2. Place your instant pot on a dry surface and open the lid.
3. Press SAUTE; add the oil and heat it.
4. Mix in the onions; cook until soft and translucent.
5. Add the ginger and garlic and sauté till fragrant.
6. Add the vegetables, yogurt, and garam masala and cook until the mixture turns almost dry.
7. Add rice, water, and salt.
8. Close the lid and check that it's sealed properly.
9. Press RICE; set timer to 10 minutes.
10. The instant pot will start building pressure; allow the mixture to cook for the set time.
11. After the timer reaches zero, turn venting knob from sealing to the venting position. Wait until float valve drops (1-2 minutes).
12. Open the lid and fluff the rice.
13. Add mint levels and cashews.
14. Stir and serve with some extra yogurt.

Mushroom Cauliflower Risotto:

Serves: 2
Preparation Time: 10 minutes
Cooking Time: 15 minutes
Macros per serving:

Calories: 300
Protein: 11 grams
Fat: 18 grams
Carbohydrates: 29 grams

Ingredients:

- 1 ½ clove, minced
- 1 tablespoon soy sauce
- 1 tablespoon tapioca starch
- ½ bone, chicken, or vegetable broth
- ½ cup of full-fat coconut milk
- ½ medium head cauliflower, cut into florets
- ½ pound small shiitake mushrooms, sliced or cremini or white mushrooms
- ½ small onion, diced
- ½ tablespoon coconut oil or ghee
- ¼ teaspoon sea salt or more, to taste
- 1/8 cup shredded cheese
- Chopped parsley, for garnish
- Ground black pepper to taste

How to make it:

1. Turn the cauliflower florets into rice-like pieces using a cheese grater or a food processor with the grater attachment.
2. Put the oil in the inner pot, making sure to coat the bottom. Set the IP to SAUTE. Heat for 5 minutes.
3. Add the mushrooms, garlic, and onion. Sauté for 7 minutes until the mushrooms are tender and have sweat, stirring frequently.
4. Add the soy sauce. Stir and cook for 5 minutes or until the vegetables are browned. Turn off the IP.
5. Add the cauliflower rice, milk, broth cheese, and salt. Stir to combine. Lock the lid and close the pressure valve.
6. Set the IP to MANUAL high pressure for 2 minutes. QPR when the timer beeps.
7. Open the lid. Sprinkle the starch on the risotto. Stir until the mixture is thick. Season with salt as needed. Add the pepper if using. Serve garnished with parsley.

Parmesan Zoodles:

Serves: 2
Preparation Time: 5 minutes
Cooking Time: 2 minutes
Macros per serving:

Calories: 322
Protein: 13 grams
Fat: 7.6 grams
Carbohydrates: 42.29 grams

Ingredients:

- 2 large zucchinis, spiralized
- 2 tablespoons olive oil
- 3 garlic clove, diced
- ¼ cup parmesan cheese, grated
- Zest of ½ lemons
- Juice of ½ lemons
- 2 tablespoons water
- Salt, pepper, to taste
- ½ cup mozzarella, grated
- 1 tablespoon parmesan cheese, grated
- Salt, pepper to taste

How to make it:

1. Add oil instant pot and press "sauté" button ("normal" preset), wait till you see hot on the display. Add onion, mushrooms and bell pepper, cook for 3-4 minutes until soft.
2. Add pasta, broccoli, spinach, tomato sauce, water, salt and pepper, pressure "cancel" button.
3. Close the lid and switch the vent to "sealed".
4. Press "pressure cook" (manual) button, use "+" or "-"button to set the timer for 5 minutes. Use "pressure level" button to set the pressure to low.
5. Once the timer is up press "cancel" button and turns the steam release handle to "venting" position for quick release until the float valve drops down. Open the lid.
6. Add mozzarella, stir well until melted. Serve topped with parmesan cheese.

Soups & Stews Recipes

Pork Soup:

Serves: 2
Preparation time: 20 minutes
Cooking time: 30 minutes
Macros per serving:

Calories: 296
Protein: 34.2 grams
Fat: 11.1 grams
Carbohydrates: 13.3 grams

Ingredients:

- 1 tablespoon olive oil
- ½ pound ground pork
- 1 small onion, chopped
- 1 cup carrot, peeled and shredded
- 1 ½ cups cabbage, chopped
- 2 cups low-sodium chicken broth
- 1 tablespoon soy sauce
- ½ teaspoon ground ginger
- Freshly ground black pepper to taste

How to make it:

1. Place the oil within the instant pot and choose SAUTE. Add the pork and cook for 5 minutes or until browned.
2. Press CANCEL and stir in the remaining ingredients.
3. Secure the lid and cook at high pressure for 25 minutes.
4. When the cooking is complete, use a quick pressure release.
5. Serve hot.

Chicken Spiced Tropical Soup:

Serves: 2
Preparation time: 8-10 minutes
Cooking time: 40 minutes
Macros per serving:

Calories: 427
Protein: 11 grams
Fat: 17 grams
Carbohydrates: 46.5 grams

Ingredients:

- 1 garlic clove, crushed or minced
- 1 small red onion, chopped
- 1 carrot, chopped
- Lime wedges for serving
- ½ small red cabbage, chopped
- A pinch of pepper and salt
- ½ pound chicken pieces
- 1/3 pineapple, peeled and make medium size cubes
- ½ teaspoon cinnamon powder
- ½ teaspoon turmeric powder
- 1 sprigs onion, chopped
- ½ teaspoon ginger powder
- ½ teaspoon white peppercorns
- ½ tablespoon tamarind paste
- Juice from 1/3 lime

How to make it:

1. Take your 3-quart instant pot; open the top lid. Plug it and turn it on.
2. In the cooking pot area, add the carrot, red onion, chicken, salt, pepper, cabbage, garlic, peppercorns. Using a spatula, stir the ingredients.
3. Close the top lid and seal its valve.
4. Press "SOUP" setting. Adjust cooking time to 30 minutes.
5. Allow the recipe to cook for the set cooking time.
6. After the set cooking time ends, press "CANCEL" and then press "QPR (Quick Press Release)".
7. Instant pot will quickly release the pressure.
8. Open the top lid, take out the meat and shred it.
9. Add back to the mix and combine.
10. In a bowl, mix 1 tablespoon soup with tamarind paste, stir and pour into the potting mix.
11. Mix the cinnamon, ginger, turmeric, pineapple and lime juice; stir the mix.
12. Press "SAUTE" setting and cook for 10 minutes more.
13. Ladle into bowls, top with the sprigs onion, on top and serve with lime wedges on the side.

Crab Sherry Soup:

Serves: 2
Preparation time: 5 minutes
Cooking time: 20-22 minutes
Macros per serving:

Calories: 434
Protein: 27 grams
Fat: 24 grams
Carbohydrates: 22.6 grams

Ingredients:

- 1 cup milk
- 1 tablespoon dry sherry
- 1 cup crab meat, flaked
- 1 cup half and half
- 2 tablespoons water
- 1 tablespoon cornstarch
- 1/8 teaspoon ground nutmeg
- 1½ tablespoons butter
- 1 strip lemon peel
- 1/3 cup crushed crackers (optional)
- Black pepper and salt, to taste

How to make it:

1. In a bowl, thoroughly mix the cornstarch and water
2. Place your instant pot on a dry surface.
3. Open the lid; add the listed ingredients except for the sherry, crackers and cornstarch mix. Stir to combine using a wooden spatula.
4. Close the lid and confirm it's sealed properly.
5. Press SOUP; set timer to 15 minutes.
6. The instant pot will start building pressure; allow the mixture to cook for the set time.
7. After the timer reaches zero, turn venting knob from sealing to the venting position. Wait until valve drops (1-2 minutes).
8. Add cornstarch mixture and sherry.
9. Press SAUTE; simmer the mixture to thicken.
10. Serve with crushed crackers on top, if using.

Creamy Wild Rice mushroom Soup

Serves: 2
Preparation time: 15 minutes
Cooking time: 45 minutes

Macros per serving:

Calories: 320
Protein: 10 grams
Fat: 13 grams
Carbohydrates: 41 grams

Ingredients:

For the IP:
- 4 ounces fresh mushrooms, sliced
- 2 stalks celery, chopped
- 2 medium carrots, chopped
- 2 cups vegetable or chicken broth
- 2 cloves garlic, minced
- ¼ teaspoon dried thyme
- ¼ onion, chopped
- ½ teaspoon salt
- ½ teaspoon poultry seasoning
- ½ cup uncooked wild rice

For the stovetop:
- ¼ cup flour
- 3 tablespoon butter
- ¾ cups of milk

How to make it:

1. Put all of the ingredients in the inner pot. Set the IP to MANUAL high pressure for 45 minutes. QPR when the timer beeps. Turn the pot off.
2. When the soup is cooked, put the butter in the saucepan and melt. Whisk in the flour and cook for 1 to 2 minutes to remove the floury flavor. Slowly whisk the milk in until the sauce is thick. Season with salt as needed.
3. Open the pot lid. Add the sauce and stir to mix well.

Notes: If you want in your dish, you can add chicken with the rest of the IP ingredients. Just shred it when cooked and stir to incorporate with the rest of the ingredients.

Chicken Mushroom Garlic Soup:

Serves: 3-4
Preparation time: 5 minutes
Cooking time: 25 minutes
Macros per serving:

Calories: 216
Protein: 24 grams
Fat: 11 grams
Carbohydrates: 5.4 grams

Ingredients:

- ½ pound chicken meat, cooked, shredded
- 2 tablespoons olive oil
- 1 onion, chopped
- 1 carrot, diced
- ½ celery, diced
- 7 oz. mushrooms, sliced
- 5 cups chicken stock
- 2 garlic cloves, chopped
- 1 teaspoon thyme
- 1 teaspoon rosemary
- 2 bay leaves
- Salt and pepper to taste

How to make it:

1. Add oil to instant pot and press "sauté" button ("normal" preset), wait till you see hot on the display. Add carrots and onion, cook for 2-3 more minutes. Add garlic, celery, and mushrooms and cook for 3 more minutes.
2. Press "cancel" button and add chicken to the instant pot, also stock, thyme, rosemary, bay leaves, Salt and pepper.
3. Close the lid, and switch the vent to "sealed".
4. Press "soup/broth" button and adjust to "less" preset. Once the timer is up press "cancel" button and turns the steam release handle to "venting" position for quick release until the float valve drops down.
5. Open the lid.

Note: You can refrigerate leftovers for later use. Simply reheat until warm (add water, if needed) and serve.

Marinara Turkey Soup:

Serves: 2
Preparation time: 8-10 minutes
Cooking time: 11 minutes
Macros per serving:

Calories: 309
Protein: 16 grams
Fat: 16.5 grams
Carbohydrates: 23 grams

Ingredients:

- ½ pound turkey, ground
- ½ tablespoon olive oil
- ½ cup cauliflower florets
- 1 garlic clove, crushed or minced
- ½ cup yellow onion, chopped
- ½ cabbage head, chopped
- 10 ounces marinara sauce
- 1 cup of water
- 2 cups chicken stock

How to make it:

1. Take your 3-quart instant pot; open the top lid. Plug it and turn it on.
2. Press "SAUTE" setting and the pot will start heating up.
3. Add the oil, turkey, garlic, and onion, stir and sauté for 5 minutes.
4. Add the cauliflower, stock, water, marinara sauce and cabbage; stir gently.
5. Close the top lid and seal its valve.
6. Press the "MANUAL" setting. Adjust cooking time to 6 minutes.
7. Allow the recipe to cook for the set cooking time.
8. After the set cooking time ends, press "CANCEL" and then press "QPR (Quick Pressure Release)".
9. Instant pot will quickly release the pressure.
10. Open the top lid; add the cooked recipe mix in serving bowls.
11. Serve and enjoy!

Chicken Pasta Soup:

Serves: 2
Preparation time: 5 minutes
Cooking time: 15 minutes
Macros per serving:

Calories: 581
Protein: 16 grams
Fat: 20.3 grams
Carbohydrates: 32.7 grams

Ingredients:

- 1 small onion, chopped
- 1 carrot, chopped
- 1 medium potato, chopped
- ½ cup pasta
- 3 cups of water
- ¾ pound chicken pieces
- 1 rib celery, chopped
- 10 green beans, strung, make small pieces
- 1 tablespoon Italian seasoning
- Salt to taste

How to make it:

1. Place your instant pot on a dry surface.
2. Open the lid, add the listed ingredients, and stir to combine using a wooden spatula.
3. Close the lid and ensure it's sealed properly.
4. Press SOUP; set timer to 15 minutes.
5. The instant pot will start building pressure; allow the mixture to cook for the set time.
6. After the timer reaches zero, wait for the float valve to drop. It will take 8-10 minutes.
7. Open the lid and transfer the food to a large bowl.
8. Divide among serving bowls; serve warm.

Beef & Potato Stew:

Serves: 2
Preparation time: 15 minutes
Cooking time: 45 minutes
Macros per serving:

Calories: 509
Protein: 43.7 grams
Fat: 15.4 grams
Carbohydrates: 47.8 grams

Ingredients:

- 1 tablespoon olive oil
- ½ pound beef stew meat, cut into cubes
- 1 small onion, chopped
- 2 carrots, peeled and chopped
- 2 medium potatoes, chopped
- 1 celery stalk, chopped
- 1 cup fresh kale leaves, Trimmed and chopped
- 1 ½ cups beef broth
- 1 tablespoon hot sauce
- ½ teaspoon garlic powder
- Salt and pepper to taste

How to make it:

1. Place the oil within the instant pot and choose SAUTE. Add the beef and cook for about 4-5 minutes or until browned.
2. Press CANCEL and stir in remaining ingredients.
3. Secure the lid, pressure the MEAT/STEW button, and use the default time of 40 minutes.
4. When the cooking is complete, does a quick pressure release.
5. Serve hot.

Cream Chicken Stew:

Serves: 2
Preparation time: 5 minutes
Cooking time: 10 minutes
Macros per serving:

Calories: 561
Protein: 17 grams
Fat: 44.7 grams
Carbohydrates: 14.3 grams

Ingredients:

- ¾ cup heavy cream
- 2 tablespoons butter
- 2 chicken thighs cut into bite-size pieces
- ¾ cup tomato sauce
- ½ tablespoon ginger, grated
- ½ tablespoon chili powder
- 1 small yellow onion, finely chopped
- 2 cloves garlic, minced
- ½ teaspoon cumin
- Black pepper and salt, to taste

How to make it:

1. Place your instant pot on a dry surface and open the lid.
2. Press Sauté; add the butter and melt it.
3. Mix in the onion, salt, and chicken; cook for 5 minutes.
4. Mix in the cream, tomato sauce, ginger, chili powder, cumin, a pinch black pepper (ground) and salt.
5. Close the lid and certify it's sealed properly.
6. Press MANUAL; set timer to 5 minutes.
7. The instant pot will start building pressure; allow the mixture to cook for the set time.
8. After the timer reaches zero, turn venting knob from sealing to the venting position. Wait until float valve drops (1-2 minutes).
9. Open the lid and transfer the food to a plate.
10. Divide among serving plates/bowls; serve warm.

Weeknight Easy Pork Stew:

Serves: 2
Preparation time: 20 minutes
Cooking time: 40 minutes
Macros per serving:

Calories: 790
Protein: 66 grams
Fat: 40 grams
Carbohydrates: 46 grams

Ingredients:

- 7 ounces canned full fat coconut milk
- 7 ounces canned diced fire-roasted or regular tomatoes
- 3 carrots or butternut squash of the same amount, peeled and chopped
- ½ teaspoon minced fresh ginger
- ½ tablespoon salt
- ½ tablespoon cumin
- ½ pound string beans, cut into 1-inch pieces
- ½ onion, diced
- 1 cup pork or chicken broth
- 1 cloves garlic, minced
- 1 ½ tablespoon curry powder
- 1 ½ pounds country-style ribs or pork shoulder
- 1 ½ medium celeriac bulbs, peeled, chopped or 3 sticks celery, chopped)
- Sea salt and pepper to taste
- Small handful chopped fresh cilantro for garnish

How to make it:

1. Put the pork in a large bowl. Add the salt, cumin, ginger, and curry powder, and mix well.
2. Except for the pepper, salt, and cilantro, add the pork mixture and the rest of the ingredients in the inner pot.
3. Lock the lid and close the pressure valve. Turn on the IP and set it to STEW.NPR when the timer beeps. Taste and add pepper and salt to taste.
4. Serve garnished with cilantro. If you desire a thick sauce, stir in arrowroot starch and stir to incorporate well.
5. You can add chopped fresh spinach once the stew is cool for a crunchy texture.

Mexican Bean Beef Stew:

Serves: 3-4
Preparation time: 5 minutes
Cooking time: 10 minutes

Macros per serving:

Calories: 551
Protein: 55.2 grams
Fat: 15.5 grams
Carbohydrates: 34.3 grams

Ingredients:

- 1 lb. ground beef
- 1 teaspoon olive oil
- 1 onion, chopped
- 2 garlic cloves, minced
- 1 tablespoon taco seasoning
- 1 jar (15 oz.) black beans, rinsed and drained
- 1 jar diced tomatoes
- 2 cups of corn frozen
- 4 cups beef broth
- 2 teaspoons lime juice
- 1 teaspoon chili powder
- 1 teaspoon ground cumin
- 4 tablespoons sour cream
- ½ cup cheddar, cheese, shredded
- Salt, pepper, to taste

How to make it:

1. Add oil to instant pot and press "sauté" button ("normal" preset,) wait till you see hot on the display. Add beef and cook for about 5-7 minutes.
2. Drain extra grease from the pot. Add onion and garlic, cook for 3 more minutes.
3. Press "cancel" and add beans, tomatoes, corn, taco seasoning, and chili powder. Ground cumin, salt, pepper, and broth.
4. Close the lid, and switch the vent to "sealed". Press "pressure cook" (manual) button, use "+" or "-"button to set the timer for 5 minutes.
5. Use "pressure level" button to set the pressure to high. Once the timer is up, press the "cancel" button and allow the pressure to be released naturally until the float valve drops down.
6. Open the lid.
7. Add lime juice; serve with sour cream and cheddar cheese on top.

Notes: You can refrigerate leftovers for later use. Simply reheat until warm (add water, if needed) and serve.

Spicy Sausage Stew:

Serves: 2
Preparation time: 5 minutes
Cooking time: 30 minutes

Macros per serving:

Calories: 491
Protein: 24.8 grams
Fat: 31.7 grams
Carbohydrates: 26.3 grams

Ingredients:

- 14 ounces canned tomato
- 7 ounces tomato puree
- 4 Italian sausages
- 2 bell peppers, sliced
- ½ tablespoon olive oil
- 2 cloves garlic, minced
- ½ cup of water
- ½ tablespoon Italian seasoning
- Black pepper and salt, to taste

How to make it:

1. Place your instant pot on a dry surface and open the lid.
2. Press SAUTE; add the oil and heat it.
3. Mix in the sausage; cook to soften for 2-3 minutes on each side.
4. Add the bell peppers, tomatoes, tomato puree, water, Italian seasoning, garlic, a pinch black pepper (ground) and salt.
5. Close the lid and ensure it's sealed properly.
6. Press MANUAL; set timer to 25 minutes.
7. The instant pot will start building pressure; allow the mixture to cook for the set time.
8. After the timer reaches zero, turn venting knob from sealing to the venting position. Wait until float valve drops (1-2 minutes).
9. Open the lid and transfer the food to a plate.
10. Divide among serving plates/bowls; serve warm.

Beef and Barley Stew:

Serves: 2
Preparation time: 10 minutes
Cooking time: 30 minutes

Macros per serving:

Calories: 800
Protein: 40 grams
Fat: 42 grams
Carbohydrates: 63 grams

Ingredients:

- 1 1/3 cup beef stock or broth
- 1 1/3 ounces mushrooms, diced
- ½ teaspoon kosher salt divided
- 1/3 bay leaf
- 1/3 cup pearl barley
- 1/3 small sweet onion, diced
- 1/3 tablespoon Worcestershire sauce
- 1/3-1/2 pound cubed stew meat
- ¼ all-purpose cup flour
- 1/8-1/4 teaspoon fresh cracked black pepper
- ¾ medium carrot, diced
- ¾ tablespoon vegetable oil
- ¾ teaspoon fresh or 1/3 teaspoon dry thyme

How to make it:

1. Put the flour, 1/8 teaspoon salt, and pinch black pepper in a re-sealable bag. Add the beef. Seal the bag.
2. Toss until the meat is coated. Set the IP to SAUTE. Put the oil in the inner pot.
3. When hot, add your beef and cook until all the sides are brown, cooking in batches as needed. Put the browned beef on a plate. Set aside.
4. Put the mushroom, carrot, and onion in the pot. Cook for 3 to 4 minutes, occasionally stirring.
5. Put the broth in the pot to deglaze, scraping the browned bits off the pot. Add the rest of the ingredients.
6. Lock the lid and close the pressure valve. Set the IP to MEAT/STEW for 25 minutes. NPR when the timer beeps. Serve.

Chili Honey Pork Stew:

Serves: 2
Preparation time: 5 minutes
Cooking time: 25 minutes
Macros per serving:

Calories: 390
Protein: 25.6 grams
Fat: 23.9 grams
Carbohydrates: 16.1 grams

Ingredients:

- ½ pound pork ribs, bone-in
- 2 tablespoons oil
- 1 onion, chopped
- 1 carrot, chopped
- 2 garlic cloves, chopped
- 1 can green chilis, diced
- 1 tablespoon apple cider vinegar
- 1 tablespoon honey
- 3 cups beef broth
- Salt, pepper, to taste

How to make it:

1. Season pork ribs with salt and pepper. Add oil to instant pot and press "sauté" button ("normal" preset), wait until you see hot on the show. Add onions and garlic, cook for 2-3 minutes stirring constantly.
2. Add pork ribs and cook for 3-4 more minutes until slightly until brown. Press "cancel" button.
3. Add broth, carrot, green chilis, apple cider vinegar, honey, salt, and pepper.
4. Close the lid, and switch the vent to "sealed".
5. Press the "meat/stew" button and suits "less" predetermined. Once the timer is up press "cancel" button and turns the steam release handle to0 "venting" position for quick release, until the float valve drops down.
6. Open the lid serve warm.

Lamb Leg Stew with Cinnamon and Dates:

Serves: 2
Preparation time: 10 minutes
Cooking time: 1 hour 40 minutes

Macros per serving:

Calories: 130
Protein: 2 grams
Fat: 4 grams
Carbohydrates: 23 grams

Ingredients:

- 7-8 medium garlic cloves, whole, peeled
- 1 teaspoon coriander powder
- 6-7 dried dates
- 1 teaspoon cumin powder
- 3 bay leaves
- 1 teaspoon turmeric powder
- 1 teaspoon salt
- 1 teaspoon ginger powder or 4 fresh sliced ginger root
- 1 teaspoon cinnamon or 1 cinnamon stick
- 1 teaspoon black pepper
- 1 tablespoon tomato paste
- 1 tablespoon tapioca, arrowroot, or cornflour, for thickening
- 1 tablespoon coconut oil
- 1 tablespoon lemon juice, or red wine or balsamic vinegar
- 1 red onion, sliced
- 1 pound lamb leg (bone out or in)
- 1 cup of water
- 1 chicken stock cube
- Couscous or rice for serving

How to make it:

1. Rub the lamb with the turmeric powder, coriander seed, cumin, pepper, and salt. Set the IP to SAUTE more modes. Put the oil in the inner pot.
2. When hot, put the lamb and fry the top and bottom for 2 to 3 minutes. Turn to the sides. Add the ginger and onion around the lamb.
3. Cook the meat for a minute for each side, stirring the ginger and onion few times. Transfer the lamb to a plate.
4. Put the remaining ingredients in the pot, mix, and boil. Press the CANCEL key. Return the lamb to the pot, setting them in the broth.
5. Lock the IP lid and close the pressure valve. Set the IP to high-pressure MANUAL for 80 minutes.

6. NPR for 6 minutes when the timer beeps, then QPR. Open the lid. Carefully transfer the lamb to a clean cutting board.
7. Set the IP to SAUTE. Simmer the broth for about 10 minutes, occasionally stirring. Slice the meat off the bone. Shred into pieces.
8. When the broth is slightly reduced after 10 minutes, add the shredded lamb in the pot. Dissolve a couple of tablespoons starch in water.
9. Whisk into the broth until glossy and thick. Turn the IP off. Serve the lamb with couscous or rice.

CONCLUSION:

Thank you for reading this book and having the patience to try the recipes.

I do hope that you gain as much enjoyment reading and experimenting with the meals as I have had writing these books.

If you would like to leave a comment, you can do it at the Order section->Digital order send and also buy paperback, in your Amazon account.

Stay safe and healthy!

www.ingramcontent.com/pod-product-compliance
Lightning Source LLC
LaVergne TN
LVHW060153240225
804387LV00008B/206